Working with Deaf Pupils

Sign Bilingual Policy into Practice

Pamela Knight and Ruth Swanwick

David Fulton Publishers

David Fulton Publishers Ltd
The Chiswick Centre, 414 Chiswick High Road, London W4 5TF

www.fultonpublishers.co.uk

British Library Cataloguing in Publication Data
A catalogue record for this book is available from the British Library.

ISBN 1–85346–793–6

Typeset by Mark Heslington, Scarborough, North Yorkshire
Printed and bound in Great Britain

Contents

The Authors

Both Pamela Knight and Ruth Swanwick are lecturers in the School of Education at the University of Leeds, where they are responsible for the postgraduate distance-learning course for training teachers of the deaf. Sign bilingual policy and practice is a central focus of this course. They are both qualified teachers of the deaf. Pamela has a particular interest in the nature of sign bilingual support in the early years and Ruth in sign bilingual language and literacy development.

Acknowledgements

The authors would like to thank all those teachers who have contributed to this book through discussion and the answering of questionnaires, and particularly Education Leeds and Thorn Park School for the Deaf in Bradford.

Preface

The impetus for this book has been a response to the growing interest in and development of the use of sign language in the education of deaf children. Educational approaches which reflect this are currently referred to as sign bilingual. The use of this term recognises the bilingual and bicultural potential of deaf children who use sign language but also emphasises the different modalities (sign, speech and text) involved.

Our perception has been, over recent years as trainers of teachers of the deaf, that innovative, sign bilingual practice continues to develop. We feel that there is a need for a book which documents the development of such sign bilingual practice. In writing this book we have undertaken to record the development of sign bilingual education and current issues in practice and research in the UK. We are aware that there are many individual examples of interesting and creative work in schools and services, and this book aims to draw these together.

There will always be deaf children for whom sign language will play a significant role in their daily lives at home, at school and beyond. At the same time, increasing sophistication of technology will clearly enhance deaf children's potential for spoken language development. We see these two factors as complementary, ultimately enhancing the linguistic and educational potential of deaf children.

The planned and focused use of sign language and developing technology should enable deaf children to develop as strong, competent and confident bilinguals.

Abbreviations

AO	aural/oral
BATOD	British Association of Teachers of the Deaf
BM	bimodal
BSL	British Sign Language
EAL	English as an additional language
ESL	English as a second language
MCE	manually coded English
SB	sign bilingual
SE	signed English
SL	sign language
SSE	sign supported English
TC	total communication
TOD	teacher of the deaf

Introduction

This book aims to explore the development of sign bilingual educational policy and practice within the wider context of bilingualism. It will look specifically at how practice is developing in classrooms in a variety of educational settings and will offer practical support as well as insight into relevant research.

Who is sign bilingualism for?

Throughout this book it is assumed that all deaf pupils will benefit from the use of sign language to some degree, in their linguistic, educational and social development, depending on their linguistic needs and preferences. When developing a language all deaf children should have access to both a signed language and a spoken language from which their first or preferred language may develop.[1] As trainers of teachers of the deaf the authors consider that all teachers of deaf children should feel confident to work within a sign bilingual or total communication teaching environment and with all deaf pupils. The exception to this would be those children with a hearing loss which is measurable but not so great as to adversely affect their development of spoken language. From this standpoint, all aspects of deaf children's language development and education can be addressed from a bilingual perspective. Sign bilingualism is considered as a framework which is inclusive of the needs of all deaf children, whatever their preferred language or level of hearing loss.

What is the purpose of the book?

The formalisation of the use of sign language and English in the linguistic and educational development of deaf children has been growing in the UK since the

[1] A language is referred to as a *first* language when it is that of the home environment, and as a *preferred* language when it is that which would most easily be developed to a level appropriate to age and stage of development.

1980s. The term sign bilingualism was coined in the late 1990s and is now an accepted term for an approach to the education of deaf children which includes the use of both the visual gestural language of the deaf community and the auditory spoken language of the hearing community. After much discussion and consultation a document was produced in 1998 – M. Pickersgill and S. Gregory, *Sign Bilingualism: A Model* – which described a model of sign bilingual education. It set out clearly the philosophy, policy and practice of sign bilingualism. Since then many services, schools for the deaf and individual schools and classes have adopted a sign bilingual approach. At one end of the continuum whole schools and services have adopted this approach, while at the other it may be an isolated teacher who has deaf children or an individual deaf child in their class. Many schools and services would suggest that they are working within a total communication philosophy but may, within that, be adopting a sign bilingual approach for some of their pupils.

The aim of this book is to draw together what might be considered current practice in diverse educational settings, then to consider what it is realistically possible to accomplish, and how teachers are able to interpret this ideal in the current educational climate of limited resources, national curriculum and shortage of staff. Also it will present and analyse some of the contemporary and relevant research in order that this area may continue to develop with the greater knowledge and understanding of all involved.

Who is the book for?

The book is initially intended for those teachers who are working in sign bilingual and total communication settings. The intention is to discuss common features and to address practically some of the issues related to delivering a sign bilingual programme. It will also be of use and interest to teachers who find themselves working in those situations but have little or no previous knowledge or experience. Mainstream teachers working in resourced schools or schools with units attached, and other involved professionals who are working with deaf children, will also find here a theoretical and practical introduction to the practice of sign bilingualism.

The book is an essential reader for teachers of the deaf in training as it explores the theoretical underpinning to sign bilingualism as well as reflecting current practice.

Structure and content of the book

The starting point for this book is a common understanding of bilingualism in general and of the specific terminology and definitions which relate to this area.

This will lead into discussions of sign bilingualism within the deaf educational context.

Part I considers the background to spoken bilingualism and how this relates to the current position of sign bilingualism. The first chapter introduces general bilingual issues and highlights their relevance to deafness and sign bilingualism and the subsequent chapters in this part consider the development of bilingual education and construction of a bilingual policy. Part II considers the early years context, looking at early intervention strategies and support at the foundation stage. Here, issues for both the family and the child are explored as well as the nature of early years sign bilingual support.

Part III moves specifically into the classroom, including language use, literacy development and developing writing skills. Finally, ongoing issues for all those involved in sign bilingual education are discussed. Throughout the whole book the intention is to take a realistic view of the practicalities of delivering a sign bilingual programme and to share common practice as it is experienced in the classroom.

PART I

Background to Bilingualism

there does not exist a universally accepted definition of bilingualism . . . bilingualism can be viewed as a continuum that includes people who may vary considerably in their linguistic knowledge, fluency and age at which they acquire each language.

(Parasnis 1996: 4)

CHAPTER 1

An Introduction to Bilingualism

Introduction

This chapter, and indeed the whole book, aims to explore the growth and development of sign bilingual policy and practice within the wider context of bilingualism. The issues to be covered will be particularly relevant for teachers working in sign bilingual settings or developing sign bilingual practice. This book is based on the assumption that all deaf pupils gain some benefit from the use of sign language in their education, to some degree. The degree depends upon their linguistic needs and preferences. All teachers of deaf children should feel confident working within a sign bilingual or total communication teaching environment and be able to communicate effectively with deaf pupils and adults. In the context of this book, deaf children's education is therefore addressed entirely from a bilingual perspective, as it is considered that this framework is inclusive of the needs of all deaf children, whatever their preferred language or level of hearing loss.

The starting point for this chapter is a common understanding of bilingualism in general and of specific terminology and definitions relating to this area. This will lead into discussions of sign bilingualism within the deaf educational context. To set the scene, this chapter introduces general bilingual issues and highlights their relevance to deafness and sign bilingualism.

Sign bilingualism within the wider bilingual context

Bilingualism, that is the use of two languages, is an integral part of human behaviour. With increasing contact and movement between cultures on a global scale, bilinguals already outnumber monolinguals and it is expected that this trend will continue in the twenty-first century. The word bilingual describes individuals who have varying degrees of proficiency and can interchangeably use two or more languages to varying degrees. It is within this broad definition that deaf people who use sign language and English have begun to be accepted as part of the wider bilingual community. This has driven the development of appropriate educational provision for bilingual deaf children.

Up until now the theoretical model which has been used to understand sign bilingualism and plan sign bilingual education has been based on research into bilingualism in two spoken languages. The major principles include a focus on the children's development of their home or first language and the transferability of skills between a first and second language. Sign bilingual education has also drawn upon the more recent positive view of bilingualism in general, particularly the advantages of being bilingual. This does provide a starting point, but sign bilingualism presents a number of separate issues which need to be explored beyond this 'best fit' framework.

In most examples of bilingualism, the individual's two languages have a spoken and a written form, sometimes referred to as modality. Usually, the primary mode of each language is the spoken form, and the learning of the spoken form of the second language will at one level reflect the processes involved in the learning of the spoken form of the first language. Bilingual learners learning to speak their second language are therefore learning a new language within a modality with which they are already familiar. These bilingual learners also have the support of the spoken form of the second language in their learning of its written form. In sign bilingualism there is no common modality since the primary form of each language differs (speech and sign) and so to learn a spoken language in addition to a signed language requires engaging with an unfamiliar modality. Also, British Sign Language (BSL) has no established written form, and so deaf children approach literacy learning with no prior experience of reading and writing in their first language.

> Deaf students are not ESL students. The majority do not have a true first language upon entrance into school as do most ESL students. ESL students typically focus on learning one additional language whereas Deaf students must learn two.
>
> (Livingston 1997: 13)

The issues resulting from this different bilingual experience are mainly concerned with the early access that deaf children have to the two languages of sign language and English, the different nature of the two languages they are developing and the implications of these two factors for English literacy development. So research into hearing bilingual learning and experience provides a framework for us to consider sign bilingualism, but the differences between deaf and hearing bilingualism must be recognised.

Definitions of bilingualism

There is an array of definitions of 'bilingual' which range from a 'native-like competence' in two languages to 'a minimal proficiency in a second language'. Many definitions are in fact problematic, either because the terms are not clearly defined (what does native-like mean?) or because they only refer to one aspect of bilingualism (such as proficiency) and ignore social and cultural issues. Linguists now agree that to try to define bilingualism as a phenomenon in isolation is meaningless since language does not exist outside the function it serves. Bilingualism is therefore entirely relative to each individual. Individual bilingualism will vary according to individual knowledge and use of each language, the extent to which individuals alternate between their two languages and the different ways in which one language influences the use of the other.

A more useful way to define individual bilingualism is to draw up a description or *bilingual profile* which considers individual language skills, cultural identities and routes to bilingualism.

Individual language skills

A bilingual person is rarely equally fluent in both languages. They usually speak one language better than the other or use the two languages for different purposes in different situations. A description which takes these factors into account will therefore be more complex but more realistic. We need to know what levels of skill the individual has in speaking, reading and writing in both languages and when, with whom and for what communicative purpose does the individual use either language?

Individual cultural identity

All languages exist within and are central to a cultural context. They are the vehicle for communicating shared experiences, values and beliefs of a group. A bilingual person has to interact with both cultures and so may also be *bicultural* to some degree, although this will vary between individuals. We might ask how familiar is the individual with both cultures and to what extent do they identify with them. Conversely, the extent to which the individual is identified by the speakers of both languages as part of their culture is also important.

Individual routes to bilingualism

Each individual child's experience of language learning, and external factors which influence this process, will shape their bilingualism and biculturalism. This accounts for the differences between bilingual individuals and helps us to understand how differing circumstances can affect the nature and type of individual bilingualism. The background and contextual information would include the circumstances in which the individual has learnt or is learning two languages and the environmental factors influencing the individual's continued development and support of both languages.

Measuring bilingualism

Measures of bilingualism are problematic since comparing language competence in two languages requires measures of language competence in each language which are comparable. One approach which avoids this problem of directly comparing the behaviour in one language with that in another involves comparing each of the bilingual person's languages with native speaker standards. By doing this we assess competence in both languages compared to that of a native speaker. This gives us one indication of the balance of their bilingualism. Exactly what types of measures are appropriate to find this sum of two monolingual behaviours is also a controversial issue since there is no one agreed test to measure language competence.

Looking at the two languages separately does give us some useful information, but we also need to understand more about each individual's bilingual behaviours, such as ways in which they move between and mix their two languages. To capture the state of individual bilinguality at present largely involves description of groups or individuals, since there are no adequate measures and existing procedures need refining. Nevertheless there is still a drive to develop effective measures and linguists would argue that to use what is available, although crude, is preferable to rejecting the notion of evaluation and measurement altogether.

For deaf pupils and the measurement of sign bilingual proficiency these problems also apply. With regard to the separate assessment of both languages there are now some measures for assessing deaf children's BSL development, although these are fairly limited in their scope. Practitioners are currently also concerned with the appropriate assessment of English abilities since school standards are designed for English first language users and many deaf pupils are learning English as an additional language with an emphasis on literacy skills. As with other bilingual children, the development of effective profiling systems seems to be a useful way forward. A full profile of a child's sign bilingualism would consider the interaction between the child's two languages and how the child manipulates two languages and three modalities (spoken, written and signed) as well as their separate abilities in either sign language or English. Later chapters in this book will illustrate the fact that deaf children's sign bilingual language ability amounts to more than the sum of their separate skills in BSL and English and should be assessed in a way which recognises their skills within, between and across the language domains.

Bilingual language development

Within the study of bilingual language development, one of the key questions is the extent to which bilingual language development is different from monolingual language development. A second is whether or not the stages of bilingual language development coincide with monolingual language development. Although there have been numerous case studies of individual bilingual children, firm conclusions cannot always be drawn about general bilingual development from these. An analysis of the research available suggests that some aspects of bilingual language development closely follow a monolingual pattern. In terms of language production, bilingual children produce their first word at the same time as monolingual children. The development of grammatical structures has also been found, in general, to be parallel, although in some studies bilingual children have been found to acquire certain grammatical structures in advance of monolinguals.

In summary, bilingual language development is not delayed compared to monolingual language development and there is no developmental or linguistic disadvantage; however, there are some characteristics of linguistic behaviour which are specific to the bilingual speaker.

Characteristics of bilingual language development

Children in a bilingual environment develop perceptual skills which enable them to tune in to the different sounds of two languages (phonology), and discriminate between them from as young as four to eight months. This development of two phonological systems facilitates the individual's ability to discriminate between two languages from an early age and to keep them separate. Other specific behaviours of bilingual speakers include language mixing, language switching and translation.

Language mixing and language switching are communication strategies where bilingual individuals optimise their communication efficiency by calling on the whole range of their repertoire. Language switching is defined as the alternate use of two languages within the same utterance or conversation, and it occurs in the speech of children and adults. It begins to happen when the bilingual child becomes aware of speaking two different languages, and it is often a necessary part of social interaction among bilinguals. Reasons for language switching are multifaceted. One often-made assumption is that bilingual speakers move into the language where they are able to express themselves more adequately. This may be the explanation in some instances, but code-switching is also an indication of the linguistic flexibility of individuals as they adapt their language and knowledge and resources to the context and audience.

Language mixing is the insertion of single words or phrases from one language into an utterance (usually a sentence) in the other. In addition to words and phrases, the sounds or grammatical structures of one language may be mixed into an utterance in the other language. Mixing may occur where the speaker only knows the item they need in one of their languages or where there is no appropriate equivalent in the language being used. All bilingual children go through a stage of mixing which usually diminishes as they get older. Language mixing is not a sign that they are unable to cope with two languages but is part and parcel of the rich experience of becoming familiar with two languages and two cultures.

Parallels with bilingualism and deafness

In the sign bilingual context a very particular example of language mixing exists since it is possible to sign and speak at the same time. Although there are many examples of how hearing bilingual children mix material from both spoken languages, only one modality is involved. For deaf individuals, contact between English and sign language results in features from a visual-gestural language and a spoken language being mixed, resulting in what is known as contact sign. This currently used term describes the use of sign language which includes elements of both BSL and English as a result of contact and interaction between deaf and hearing people. Language mixing by deaf children shares the characteristics of that of hearing bilingual children as it is the result of the children's creative use of their linguistic resources. It is important to recognise the distinction between this type of natural language mixing and the use of contrived manually coded forms of English. This is often used for teaching purposes (bimodal communication) where some aspects of sign or speech become redundant. The contrast between the natural and contrived mixing of sign language and English and the implications for the teaching context are discussed in detail in later chapters.

Routes to bilingualism

There are many routes to becoming bilingual, which depend largely on the individual's family circumstances, their educational experiences and the wider social context. Throughout this book we are mainly concerned with children from linguistic minorities since this bilingual situation is similar to deaf children's bilingual experience. For these children, the home language or language of their parents is a minority language. Usually the minority language does not have official status, so learning the majority language may be necessary for education and future employment. These children become bilingual because they learn the majority language through school and through their interactions with the majority society. The success of this route to bilingualism, in terms of the child's sense of personal identity and their academic achievement, depends very much on the maintenance of the individual's home language. It also depends on how appropriately their second language learning (learning of the majority language) is managed in the school context.

This route to bilingualism is in parallel with that of the bilingual deaf child, in that the preferred languages of, for example, BSL or Hindi are minority languages without official status, or educational or economic value, within the majority culture. Both the deaf and the hearing child are also in the situation of learning English in the school setting, where the level of support for their home language will vary depending on educational policy.

There are however some significant differences which make the particular route a deaf child will follow both unique and at times more difficult. Most linguistic minority children acquire their first language at home and from their immediate community and begin to acquire the second language at school. For the deaf child of deaf parents this is also likely to be the pattern, and therefore a possible route to bilingualism will involve learning sign language naturally at home and English more formally in the school setting.

For the deaf child of hearing parents, the experience may be different. Hearing families of deaf children are unlikely to have sign language skills when their deaf child is born and it may be that the family are learning sign language at the same time as the child is acquiring language. For a deaf child from a hearing family therefore the route to bilingualism may involve learning sign language and English at the same time. English will still be the language of the home and it is likely that a mixture of natural sign language, manually coded and spoken and written English will be used in that environment.

Other differences concern the learning of the majority language. For the deaf child from either a deaf or a hearing family there are other factors affecting developing language competence in the spoken form of the majority language. The deaf child is learning a second language which they cannot fully hear, whereas the hearing child has access to the second language which is not limited by any physiological factor. In addition to this, because sign language is a visual-gestural language there is no written form. This means that deaf children who are fluent sign language users will still not have had the experience of the written form of their language which some other hearing bilingual children do. When bilingual deaf children are learning to read and write they are also learning about an entirely new system of communication which requires very different skills to learning the conversational form of a language. Finally, many minority language bilingual hearing children live in communities where they are surrounded by other speakers of their language. They therefore hear their language being used on a daily basis by other children and adults, which confirms that they are part of a larger group of people like themselves. Deaf families who use sign language are not generally found to live in such tight-knit communities. The onus is therefore on the educational setting to support and provide positive affirmation of deaf culture and identity.

Two languages, two cultures

An individual who uses two or more languages is also engaging with two or more cultures. Culture concerns the shared experiences, values and beliefs of a group. Language can be identified as the most significant defining feature of a culture and also as the vehicle for the communication of that culture. Cultural identity is an important aspect of personality, and the bilingual person develops a unique identity, different from that of a monolingual. A cultural identity is the way in which an individual defines himself or herself in relation to the cultures within a society.

Identification with a culture or a community is concerned with the extent to which an individual feels to be a part of that culture or community, and is able to use the language in appropriate contexts and to participate comfortably in activities or events specific to that community. A cultural identity usually involves a sense of belonging and of shared values within a group. It has been found that children by the age of six can develop some type of cultural identity in that they are able to perceive themselves as a part of a specific group. This does not mean that a child develops two cultural identities, but that they integrate both their cultures into one unique identity.

An understanding of and sensitivity towards individual cultural identity is central to successful bilingual education since it has been found that children who identify positively with both cultures are more successful language learners whereas those with a conflict of cultural identity are more likely to achieve poorly in both languages. If a child's environment supports both cultures they will be better able to develop a more harmonious bicultural identity.

Deaf people who consider themselves as socially and culturally deaf and use sign language constitute a social group not unlike a minority spoken language group. Accepting the concept of a 'deaf culture' challenges us to think beyond deafness as a disability and to consider the broader social and linguistic implications.

> Unlike other cultures, deaf culture is not associated with a single place . . . rather, it is a culture based on relationships among people for whom a number of places and associations may provide common ground.
>
> (Lane, Hoffmeister and Bahan 1996: 5)

As this quotation illustrates, the notion of deaf culture does not relate to a particular place on a map but rather to what is often referred to as the 'deaf world' where people share the experience of what it is like to be deaf. The bonds, associations and shared experiences that deaf people have developed with each other make up deaf culture. These bonds include, most importantly, a common language, but also social and political organisations, artistic and literary expression as well as a shared experience of being a minority group within a majority society.

Some argue that it is the network of residential schools for the deaf that has enabled deaf culture to survive and to be passed down through generations. It is within these schools that many deaf people have acquired their sign language skills and, often, lifelong friendships. It is argued that this environment also enables young people to develop a strong sense of deaf identity and belief in themselves, thus equipping them to function effectively in deaf and hearing communities. The strong move towards the inclusion of deaf children into mainstream schools is therefore seen by some as a threat to sign language and deaf culture and to the individual's knowledge of deaf heritage and personal deaf identity.

Advantages of being bilingual

Up until the 1960s there was a negative view of bilingualism born out of a belief that being bilingual disadvantaged the intellectual development of the individual. However, the political movement, particularly in the USA, advocating language rights, and the growth of balanced research into bilingualism, have resulted in more positive attitudes to bilingualism and an increased awareness of the advantages of being bilingual. Current research suggests that benefits for a bilingual person encompass cultural, communicative and cognitive advantages.

One potential advantage of bilingualism is that children experience two or more cultures. While most of us experience a variety of subcultures of our own culture and experience other cultures as a tourist or traveller, to actually penetrate a different culture requires the language of that culture. This wider perspective and breadth of understanding can result in greater tolerance and a less ethnocentric outlook because of the opportunity for insight into cultural differences.

Bilingual people are also advantaged because their ability to use two languages enables them to communicate with a greater number and variety of people, whether that be within the community, across the United Kingdom or internationally. Being bilingual may allow an individual to bridge the generations within a family, or on a wider scale to bridge communities and societies. Being able to move between two languages may lead to more sensitivity in communication. Bilinguals have to constantly make choices about language use and so are often more attuned to the communicative needs of others.

When two languages are relatively well-developed within an individual he or she is likely to experience thinking or cognitive advantages. Research has shown that bilingualism can have positive effects on cognitive development where both of the child's languages are respected and supported in the academic and social setting. Among the cognitive advantages identified as resulting from bilingualism is a more pronounced metalinguistic awareness. Metalinguistic awareness is defined as the ability to think about and reflect on the linguistic nature of language use. Examples of evidence of this special awareness include the individual's ability to attend to the form of the language rather than focus on the message. For example, a child who can cope with the demands of the curriculum in either language is likely to be able to separate meanings from the words themselves, to think more creatively and divergently and to be more sensitive to communication between people. This pronounced awareness of certain linguistic forms can be explained in part by bilingual children's daily experience of trying to keep their languages separate so as to avoid interference and of comparing and contrasting the grammatical structures and vocabularies of the two languages.

Some research suggests that bilingual children are not likely to experience this positive effect on their intellectual development until they reach a high degree of proficiency in both languages (Cummins's threshold hypothesis discussed in Baker 2001). If this were the case, we would not expect minority language children in transitional language programmes and deaf children who are unlikely to reach balanced bilingualism to experience these positive cognitive benefits. Is it possible for sign bilingual children to share the same reported linguistic advantages as other bilinguals? More information is needed about deaf children's ability to see their two languages as separate and to make decisions about the most appropriate way to convey the same meaning in both languages.

Bilingual individuals are further advantaged if their minority language is valued in terms of their self-esteem and sense of social identity. A child whose home language is a minority language but who finds in school that the language is disparaged by teachers by, for example, its non-use in the curriculum, may suffer in terms of self-esteem. If children's first language is rejected by the school, by implication so are their parents, their extended family, their community and their very sense of self. For those whose first language is celebrated in school, their self-esteem may be raised and strengthened. Where there is denial of sign language as the natural language of deaf people, then there can be a diminution of self-esteem and self-identity. When there is acceptance and celebration of sign language as the first language of deaf people, then self-esteem and self-identity may be supported, secured and strengthened, leading to positive outcomes in terms of achievement in the school and beyond.

Issues in bilingual education

Britain is a multilingual society and has been so for many years, during which time individuals and groups have sought to ensure that the benefits of a positive approach to bilingualism are not lost to pupils, their parents, other educators and society. However, promoting bilingualism has been a continuing struggle. Britain does not have a positive national attitude to bilingualism and learning other languages, and so multicultural education faces many challenges, the most notable challenge being the absence of adequate planning and resourcing, at a political level, for the educational needs of minority language pupils. These pupils come from a wide variety of language and literacy backgrounds and have a home language other than English; some of them are still in the process of learning to use English as an additional language for educational purposes. Some pupils operate in more than two languages. For many, contact with all members of their family provides a strong motivation for learning and maintaining the home language, although many lack opportunities to develop a full range of linguistic skills in their first language.

In the classroom the priority for bilingual pupils is access to the curriculum and to appropriate assessment procedures. The key issues are that most bilingual learners are unfamiliar with the use of standard English for academic purposes, and recently introduced literacy benchmarks and assessment regimes in schools are designed for pupils with an English-speaking background. Wider concerns which relate directly to these teaching and learning issues include language use and the role of mother-tongue teaching, the celebration of minority language and culture and appropriate funding for bilingual teaching and non-teaching staff.

A model of bilingual education

International research and practice has found that bilingual education is more effective and more successful when there is an early emphasis on the minority language, with a child becoming bilingual later. Using the child's first or preferred language can be the most efficient means of initially acquiring curriculum concepts, understanding and knowledge. For example, research from the United States has shown that children who learn through their first (minority) language for as long as possible not only tend to have improved final achievement, but also their English language skills tend to develop to a higher level than those who were taught through their second language with some first language support. While the majority language may be introduced around the age of seven or eight (and therefore bilingualism is encouraged), the child retains their minority language, works through that minority language and generally tends to achieve success. The reasons for the child achieving success may be due to the fact that the school accepts and builds upon the linguistic and intellectual resources the child already has when moving from home to school. The child's performance is usually raised as a result of their improved self-esteem and experience of learning through their first or natural language. Also and importantly, ideas, concepts and knowledge developed in the first language transfer easily to the second language.

It is also an advantage if priority is given to the development of children's bicultural skills and understanding, enabling them to achieve their potential even when the culture of the school is very different from that of the home. An active participative culture needs to accompany the minority language. Within a community, there need to be plenty of opportunities for minority language speakers to use their language which fosters a sense of pride and confidence in their culture and community. Implicit in this is the full involvement of parents and communities in school policy-making and their children's learning. This requires a partnership with parents both inside and outside the school, where parents are included in the classroom, bringing in their 'funds of knowledge', and supporting their children outside school.

The above 'enrichment' model of bilingual education can only be achieved if there are bilingual teaching and non-teaching staff, and professional development and career openings for these staff. This requires planning and resourcing at government level as well as within individual schools and services.

Conclusion

In summary, it is estimated that approximately two-thirds of the world are bilingual or multilingual. That is, the majority of the world are bilingual or multilingual and a minority are monolingual. Deaf people therefore may be considered a linguistic minority but as bilinguals they form part of the majority. This introduction has shown that there are many similarities between deaf and hearing bilingual people and that although a complete parallel between sign and spoken bilingualism cannot be drawn, deaf children can be seen as a specific group within the wider bilingual community and do share many similarities with spoken bilinguals. There are sufficient social, political and linguistic parallels to enable us to draw on general bilingual theory as a basis for the exploration of features of sign bilingualism, but educational practice needs to recognise certain differences introduced in this chapter. These include the circumstances in which deaf children acquire sign language, their access to spoken English, and their experience of literacy and of code-mixing in bilingual environments.

Many of the arguments for retaining a minority language as a child's first language and for an 'enrichment' form of bilingual education for such children also hold for deaf children. The argument that children from language minorities should become bicultural and culturally pluralistic also applies to bilingual deaf people. The following chapters will explore the development of bilingual education for deaf children, considering its origins and theoretical basis as well as current classroom practice and new directions.

Further reading

Baker, C. (2001) *Foundations of Bilingual Education and Bilingualism*, 3rd edn, Clevedon: Multilingual Matters

Parasnis, I. (ed.) (1996) *Cultural and Language Diversity and the Deaf Experience.* Cambridge: Cambridge University Press

CHAPTER 2

The Development of Sign Bilingual Education

Introduction

This chapter will look, briefly, at the historical context of deaf education and consider how the current educational scenario has developed over time. It will also look at current philosophies and policies as they are reflected in the classroom today.

In the *Directory of Establishments Educating Hearing Impaired Children and Students* (British Association of Teachers of the Deaf 2000), authorities, units and schools are requested to say which communication approach they use within their particular setting: aural/oral (AO), total communication (TC), bi-modal (BM) or sign bilingual (SB). Many use a variety of communication approaches, while others opt for two out of the three, and yet others are identified as using one specific approach to communication.

This is a very different picture from 20 years ago when information on communication policies was not available in this form. The latest directories have included this information, and it is interesting to note the growth and variety of settings which are offering SB as one, or the only, approach to communication in their service. Information from BATOD would suggest that in the order of 250 schools (44 per cent), services and individual teachers would identify sign bilingualism as their policy. Broken down this is in the order of eight schools for the deaf (25 per cent), 37 hearing impaired services and over 70 individual teachers. In all about 250 settings are identifying sign bilingualism or a bi-modal approach as their policy.

In order to establish clearly the thinking and events that have led to this gradual shift, a brief consideration should be given to the history of deaf education and the place of communication policies within that perspective.

The historical perspective

Deaf people and deaf communities have historically had a language of their own, the visual gestural language that is sign language, which has remained alive and in use through the centuries. There have been references to it as early as the fifth century BC. Sign languages have always existed as a means of communication, although there is no early recording of their use as a basis for developing literacy or in education. The earliest records of a systematic attempt to educate deaf children at all was in Spain in the sixteenth century. The honour of being the first teacher of the deaf is often accorded to Pedro Ponce de Leon (Ree 2000), who undertook the task of teaching the son of a nobleman to read, write and speak, solely in order for him to have access to his inheritance. There is no record of the methods de Leon used, but there is a suggestion that he began with reading and writing before moving on to speech and the use of finger spelling. In Great Britain in the eighteenth and nineteenth centuries teachers were credited with teaching deaf pupils both literacy and expressive and receptive spoken language skills. Many of the techniques used were kept secret, presumably for commercial reasons, and rivalry was rife between educators of the deaf.

In France the Abbé de l'Epée was also working with deaf students but was much less secretive about his methods. They were based upon the following principles. First, he believed that sign language was the natural language of deaf people and was their primary vehicle for thought and communication. Using signs from their natural language, he devised a signing system that was able to reflect the grammar of the spoken language. It could be argued that this is an early form of signed English (SE), or rather signed French. Second, he was influenced by the Spanish teacher Bonet, who advocated very early intervention in the teaching of deaf children. Third, he believed in a monolingual language environment, that is, only one language used at a time, or what is referred to as language separation, one of the major issues currently addressed in sign bilingual settings. These thoughts of early intervention, language separation and use of sign language are consistent with some of the current ideas about the education and linguistic development of deaf children.

Although de l'Epée advocated the teaching of articulation skills he felt that the disproportionate amount of time required to teach the spoken word was at the expense of developing the more important intellectual skills. He was heavily criticised for this, particularly by the German school of teachers, who were convinced of the value of teaching spoken language to deaf children as 'the natural order of learning'.

So there was, at that time-division and argument about methodology among the educators of deaf children. What is interesting to note is that most of the issues being faced today concerning the education of deaf children have been addressed, one way or another, in previous centuries.

Similarly in the United States the need to address the education of deaf children was a concern in the early 1800s. It was decided that Thomas Gallaudet should come to Europe to consider the varying methodologies in use and how best to proceed in the USA. In the event, he found difficulty in accessing the systems in Great Britain and returned to the USA with a French deaf teacher of the deaf, Laurent Clerc, a pupil of de l'Epée. Together they introduced methods of communication and education which acknowledged the place of sign language as already established in France. However, influence from Germany and the UK grew in the USA, leading to the introduction of aural/oral methods in certain areas, which instigated the ensuing debate about methodology; that is, the aural/oral method versus methods incorporating the use of sign language.

Gradually aural/oral methods gained strength and favour in both Europe and in the USA, endorsed by a conference in Milan in 1880. This advocated and led to a repression of sign language in the education of deaf children and an almost total disregard of the place of deaf teachers of deaf children. Methods advocating the use of sign language or a combination of sign and speech became less popular. This legacy of two discrete methodologies persisted well into the twentieth century.

By the 1960s there was a growing awareness both in Europe and in the USA that many deaf children were failing to develop acceptable levels of language skills or to reach their learning potential. It was seen that a significant number of deaf children were leaving school with very poor reading and writing skills. The focus of the concern became the 'oral method' then prevalent both in Europe and the USA. It was thought that it was not meeting the linguistic needs of many severely and profoundly deaf children.

Research at that time also indicated that deaf children who had deaf parents and had used sign language from an early age were achieving more highly in school and had more developed literacy skills than other deaf children. This greater success was accredited to the fact that deaf children of deaf parents were likely to have had natural and uninterrupted communication within the family, from birth. This evidence, plus the growing recognition of sign language as a true and full language which is rule-governed, shares similarities with other languages and possesses an identifiable developmental sequence, meant there could be an acceptable shift from a predominantly oral-only approach to one which might include the use of sign as a resource for communication with deaf children.

One approach, using sign as a resource, became known as total communication (TC) and was an all-embracing term which came to mean the use of any method of communication which was effective with deaf children, including speech, speech reading, use of sign, reading and writing and finger spelling. This approach is still prevalent today in many schools. These and other terms will be explored later in the chapter.

There continue to be many schools and services which work under aural/oral and TC approaches. But more recently, there has been a move towards identifying more clearly the uses and role of sign language and the sign systems which support spoken languages. This has led to a more systematic consideration of the use and place of both spoken and signed languages with deaf children, in the home and in the classroom. This identification and separate use of sign language and spoken language and the understanding of their roles in both language acquisition and education has led to the concept of a bilingual approach to the language development and education of deaf children. As the term bilingual is generally associated with the use of two or more spoken languages, the term sign bilingualism has come into common usage to encompass an approach that is using two languages that are in different modalities, i.e. the auditory/spoken mode of spoken languages and the visual gestural mode of sign languages.

Before examining more closely sign bilingualism, which is the focus of this book, it is interesting to see how the use of aural/oral and total communication approaches is currently reflected in practice.

Current practice of total communication and aural/oral approaches

A common target of aural/oral approaches is the development of spoken language and the subsequent development of literacy skills built on that language development. Also common to all aural/oral approaches is the commitment to developing residual hearing to the full, with an accompanying focus on the use of amplification systems and favourable acoustic conditions in all classrooms. The methodology by which spoken language is developed is more variable. It is always through the specific development of listening skills and spoken conversation with a more mature language user, but the basis of this conversational interaction may vary. Methodology encompasses, predominantly, the natural aural approach, the maternal reflective method or a structured aural approach. Great emphasis is placed upon early diagnosis of deafness and immediate and appropriate amplification. It is accepted that the use of natural gestures may facilitate understanding in the early years, but there is no place for the use of formalised sign within educational settings using an aural/oral approach. In general, the aural/oral approach is based on the philosophy that deaf children can learn language by the same developmental process as hearing children, if exposed consistently to spoken language.

The aim of a TC approach is initially to ensure that the communicative needs of each individual child are met. This is a child-centred approach and allows for the full spectrum of language modes to be used to achieve these ends. To define total communication as an educational approach is much harder. This is because there is a variety of definitions and a variety of interpretations in practice. The original concept of total communication was an approach incorporating all means of communication, including the use of sign, to ensure fullest possible communicative success with deaf children. All educational establishments using a TC approach have an ethos of ease of communication to meet the needs of the individual deaf child as a priority, but in reality there is wide diversity of practice under the name of TC. That is, some establishments use English, sign supported English (SSE) and BSL depending upon the context and the needs of the child, while others would more strictly use an SSE approach where signs are predominantly used alongside spoken English and the amount of signed input varies according to the needs of the child. Currently the use of the term TC has often come to mean the practice of SSE. Many places would add the caveat that although they say they are working within a TC approach they do use sign language with children for whom it is the first or preferred language, in certain circumstances.

In the context of this book it is the use of a sign bilingual approach, the use of sign language and English with deaf children, that is the focus. It is those children for whom sign language is a first or preferred language and English is a second language that the sign bilingual context is relevant. This may be in a purely SB context, or where teachers are opting for using an SB approach within a TC environment with some children. Whereas originally SB could be seen as a way of formalising the use of sign language with deaf children it is clear that while this certainly enhances linguistic development, English is also needed and has to be equally addressed as the language of literacy and of the majority community.

The challenge facing all teachers of the deaf working in these situations is how and when to use each language and, more importantly, how to manage this within the wide variety of education settings in which they are working. The focus of the rest of the book is to explore these issues.

Growth of support for sign bilingualism

Support for SB is strong around the country and the impetus for it or the 'movement towards' SB grew from the early 1980s. That is when many teachers of the deaf were becoming interested in the potential use of sign language as a linguistic and educational tool. At this time BATOD produced a policy statement suggesting that BSL did not have a role in the educational setting. They have now clearly moved away from this position, but at the time it had the effect of motivating those parents, professionals and teachers who retained an interest in the potential for SL in the classroom to form a study group which later became known as LASER (LAnguage of Sign as an Educational Resource) in 1983. The aim of LASER is to promote the use and role of BSL in the education of deaf children; particularly the bilingual option.

This group is currently reconsidering its focus and is in the process of becoming affiliated to the National Association of Language Development in the Curriculum (NALDIC). This is an organisation which focuses on the needs of all users of English as an additional language. It organises regional conferences and workshops on themes such as assessment, literacy development, curriculum development and teaching approaches.

LASER had met consistently since 1983 with a focus on conferences and workshops. The conferences have had a developmental theme moving from discussions in 1987 considering 'Educating the Deaf Child: The Bilingual Option' through to 'Sign Bilingualism: A Model' in 1998. A document was published, as a result of this, in which a clear model of sign bilingual education is described in terms of philosophy, policy and practice. This was written by Gregory and Pickersgill (1998) and was endorsed by many professionals and institutions working in the field.

As well as developing philosophy and policy, LASER has constantly tackled practical issues in workshop meetings throughout the country. These have been for teachers, parents and professionals where the practical issues of working in a bilingual setting have been raised and discussed, and ideas shared. A strength of these workshops is the immediate benefit to all participants and the consistency with which the findings and ideas raised within the workshop situation have been published and circulated.

A further strength of LASER was the open opportunity, given by the workshops and meetings, for teachers to get together and share ideas in an informal and relaxed setting. These meetings highlighted the wide variety of education and work settings from which teachers and parents were coming. Schools and services that were working positively within a bilingual setting were well represented, and many teachers and parents came from the same schools and services. Also there were teachers from more isolated settings, such as a unit within one school, or indeed teachers working on their own, sometimes with a single SL-using child in and among others. They were particularly looking to share ideas, practical suggestions and strategies for use in the classroom.

There is also a 'consortium' of schools and services who work within a bilingual policy. This is largely for teachers, and the focus is equal access to National Curriculum assessments for those pupils for whom SL is their first or preferred language. There has been a particular concentration on the administration of SATs at Key Stages 1 and 2. Also a focus of discussions has been development of appropriate teaching strategies for English, the inclusion of deaf pupils in literacy and numeracy hours and the development of appropriate assessment materials.

A further rapidly growing area for support, discussion and sharing of ideas is the internet. There is a group which can be accessed on the web, entitled 'Bilingual Education for Deaf Children', which was created in October 2000 and where 'anyone involved and/or interested in the bilingual education of deaf children can share experiences, insights, frustrations, hopes'. In less than a year the membership has grown to over 100. Discussions are lively, topical and informative. There is also a group addressing 'English as an additional language', which includes issues related to all bilingual deaf learners.

So the current picture is one of developing activity, interest and focus on a sign bilingual approach for deaf children in a variety of educational settings. That is, schools, whole services, units and individual teachers. This has implications for the training needs of teachers of the deaf, for deaf adults working in schools and nurseries, for support to families, for the roles of other professionals working in the field and for the parents and families of all deaf children. There is a continuing need for national training and networking for all teachers, not only as a separate group but as part of the whole deaf educational context.

Research evidence

A final consideration of this chapter is the research evidence related to the implementation of a sign bilingual approach and how this can reinforce the practice of sign bilingualism both for language development and in the classroom.

Research has suggested there are many advantages, both practical and personal, to having a bilingual experience. One advantage is that children can access two or more worlds of experience and deaf children have the opportunity to access both the culture of the deaf community as well as that of the hearing community. When both languages are relatively well developed the individual is likely to experience thinking and cognitive advantages. There are many parallels to be drawn between deaf and hearing bilingualism, particularly in the context of an enrichment model where children are allowed to use their minority language as long as is necessary to ensure full access to the school curriculum. (For further discussion of these issues refer to Chapter 1.)

Early research into the achievements of deaf children of deaf parents (Vernon and Koh 1970; Meadow 1968) showed that there were higher levels of success in terms of language, academic achievement and social development. These early findings meant that professionals started to regard seriously the educational use of sign language as a means of enabling deaf children to achieve linguistically and academically.

There is evidence of the positive influence on reading (Mahshie 1995) where it was found that, in a bilingual class in Sweden, deaf children were reading appropriately for their age. This was repeated in many classes where a positive programme of bilingual education was well established. Gregory (1997) concluded that children use their knowledge of BSL to inform their writing in English, and goes on to argue that this could be a useful transitional stage which could open up the possibilities for the use of BSL in discussing the grammatical structure of English.

The early experience of sign language has also been found to be facilitative in the learning of English and does not appear to interfere with, or in any way inhibit, the development of spoken or written English skills.

There is evidence of the positive effects of fluent sign language users on the play and social interaction of deaf children in both mainstream schools and nursery settings (Knight and Swanwick 1996). The presence of staff with whom children can communicate in an easy and natural way allows for the more positive development of play and role play and the accompanying interaction, and also gives children the certainty of being understood and responded to in a natural and constructive way.

An issue that has continually dogged research into the achievements of deaf children and the factors affecting it has been the tools available to the researchers. Tests used invariably depended upon the degree of skill in English and had usually been developed with hearing children in mind. This is particularly true when assessing literacy skills. Also, many tests used with deaf children had inappropriate content. It is suggested that the lives and educational experiences of deaf children may be very different from those of hearing children, and a clear understanding of this issue is required when constructing tests.

The current challenge for researchers into the language development and/or curriculum understanding of deaf children in bilingual settings is the development of valid, reliable, appropriate test materials. Also there is a current and urgent need for increased knowledge of BSL development and clear procedures for assessing this (Powers *et al.* 1998).

SB is a new and developing area in Britain and much of the research is ongoing and of necessity of a longitudinal nature, but already there is evidence of advantages for early social interaction, for the development of literacy skills and for the overall benefits of a bilingual experience.

Further reading

Gregory, S., Knight, P. *et al.* (eds) (1998) *Issues in Deaf Education*, London: David Fulton. There are three chapters describing current policies in deaf education which clearly outline the different approaches.

Lane, H. (1984) *When the Mind Hears: A History of the Deaf*, New York: Random House. This book offers a comprehensive description of the history of deaf people and deaf education in particular.

CHAPTER 3

Sign Bilingual Policy

Introduction

As discussed briefly in the preceding chapter, the development of sign bilingual policy and practice over recent years has led to the publication of a document defining 'a model of sign bilingualism' (Pickersgill and Gregory 1998). It was designed for use by those involved directly in the planning and implementation of education of deaf children and young people. The aim of that document is to

> clarify the current confusing situation in which terms (related to sign bilingualism) are used without agreed definitions

> (p. 3)

This model has been devised, first, by means of considering the philosophy that underpins sign bilingualism. In this case it is through discussion and clarification of the underlying principles associated with bilingualism; that is, bilingualism in the wider context of the use of two spoken languages as well as sign bilingualism. Second, it has been by development of a specific policy through which the practice of sign bilingualism can be identified. And, third, by the practice itself that is the process by which this end can be achieved.

This chapter goes on to consider in detail the underpinning philosophy and subsequent policy and practice that make up the 'model of sign bilingualism'. We accept that in reality this cannot be a 'cut and dried' process as there are implications for both inclusive and segregated settings, for the variety of individual needs, and in addition there are significant resource implications.

Philosophical foundation

The philosophy underpinning sign bilingualism is based on a 'linguistic and cultural minority model of deafness and a social model of disability' (Pickersgill and Gregory 1998: 3). The term model is used here to describe and explain a framework that enables society to understand, describe and interpret its own behaviours. A social model views disability in the context of the society in which the majority of people live. It focuses on an environment that has evolved around and been developed by non-disabled people. So from this perspective people are not disabled by their particular disability, but by the extent to which the social environment in which they live places constraint upon their opportunity to function fully within it. To this extent deaf people are disabled within a society where the spoken language of the community is valued and is the one which the majority of people share and use. This is also the language of literacy and the one in which the commercial and social world of the particular environment functions.

A more positive view of deaf people is through a general acceptance of the first or preferred language used by deaf people. This allows for a model of deafness that is described and explained in terms of preferred language use. This focuses not on a model of deaf people as having a particular medical condition but as members of a minority linguistic group who have a distinct language and culture. A goal of sign bilingualism is that deaf children should become bilingual and therefore bicultural and have the ability to participate both in the hearing society and in the deaf community.

It is a well-accepted concept that those who have the majority language of the society largely have the power within that society. In most societies clearly those who use the majority language are in positions of power in most aspects of government, the arts and the professions. It is a goal for sign bilingual education to ensure that deaf people have skills in both spoken and signed languages and therefore equal opportunities to partake fully in the functioning and organisation of the society in which they live.

The known advantages of bilingualism, including sign bilingualism, are explored in Chapter 1. These advantages must be exploited to the full with deaf children to ensure that they have every opportunity to reach their full potential in the society in which they live. The outcome of sign bilingual support and education should be that every deaf child should gain skills in sign language and in the majority language of their society in which they live to meet their academic and social needs as children and as adults.

Deaf identity

The opportunity to be part of the deaf community which is facilitated by, among many other things, the use of sign language, contributes to the feeling of positive identity. It is the feeling not only of a shared language but also of a shared and common experience of the world that creates a deaf identity. It has been well documented that deaf children and adults who do not have well developed sign language skills do have problems in establishing a clear identity for themselves.

The development of literacy skills

It is essential that deaf children develop good literacy and spoken language skills to their fullest possible potential. It is argued that deaf pupils' sign language skills are recognised as an area of strength in relation to their second language learning, and that these skills can provide the main route into second language development without emphasis on speech or the use of English-based signs. (Issues related to the development of literacy skills are discussed fully in Chapters 6 and 7.)

Policy and practice

A policy should ensure that a process is in place which will enable a philosophy to be translated into practice. It is not possible to separate issues of policy from practice, as the principles enshrined in a policy are worthless and ineffectual if they are not implemented in practice.

A sign bilingual policy places the role of sign language and of native sign language users at the heart of the education of deaf children. It also encompasses issues that are holistic in their approach, such as the development of a positive deaf identity, an awareness of issues related to deafness in the hearing community and a respect for the language and culture of deaf people.

It considers the organisational strategies that allow for the planned and structured use of both sign language and English.[2] Although the model is largely developed around the linguistic needs of those deaf children for whom sign language will be a first or preferred language, it also addresses the needs of those deaf children for whom spoken language is the preferred language and sign language may be their second language. This ensures that they equally have the opportunity to enhance their cognitive, academic and social opportunities.

The policy of planning language input and development on a 'continuum' of need, as identified individually, is also at the heart of a sign bilingual policy. This involves the planned use of both BSL and English in a systematic way depending upon the individual needs of the child. This may vary over time, depending upon not only the linguistic development and skills of the child but also the demands of the situation. That is, the social and literacy demands as well as the specific demands of the curriculum.

---

[2] Many of the principles outlined in this book are applicable to sign bilingualism in an international context. From now on the terms BSL and English will be used to denote sign languages and spoken languages.

Practice

In the following sections of this chapter, issues of policy and ensuing practice will be considered together. This is because they are inextricably linked and all aspects of policy should be identified for use in practice. Indeed there is a suggestion that unless all issues are evident in practice then the policy cannot be identified as truly sign bilingual. In the real world of segregated education, inclusive education, issues of preferred languages and the practicalities of resourcing provision it would be harsh in the extreme to make a judgement on absolutes.

The issues are considered in four identifiable sections: those dealing with language and communication, curriculum and assessment, staffing and links with parents and the community. First, points of policy will be outlined, followed by how these are implemented and demonstrated in practice. The lists that follow give the overall structure of the implementation of a sign bilingual policy in practice in the classroom. All areas will be expounded and explored further in the subsequent chapters in the book.

The following detailed components of policy and practice are taken from Pickersgill and Gregory 1998 and Pickersgill 1998.

Language and communication

In this section the term language is used to mean that language (BSL or English) which the individual child would most readily acquire at an age-appropriate time, and would from preference use as a basis for cognitive, emotional and academic development.[3] Policy criteria include the following issues.

Policy issues

In the list of policy issues below, emphasis is placed on establishing the roles of BSL and English within a continuum and focusing on preferred and second languages.

- Equal status is given to BSL and English. Both are regarded as languages of education.
- Pre-school intervention and support programmes include the planned use of both BSL and English to ensure timely opportunities for their age-appropriate acquisition.

---

[3] Sometimes the term first language is used, but there are, by implication, issues related to the language of the home, so the term preferred language is used throughout as more indicative of individual children's needs.

- Either BSL or English is considered as preferred language and the aim of age-appropriate competence is crucial.
- Decisions made regarding family support and educational placement are made in response to the child's developing linguistic profile.
- Variation in children's language dominance and skills is acknowledged and respected.
- The interdependence of BSL and English and the transference of skills between them is encouraged.
- The aim should be that use of sign language and English (spoken and written) is kept separate.
- The place of pidgin sign varieties (as naturally occurring contact forms) and manually coded English (and other contrived systems) should be defined and specified.

Practice

The issues of practice are dominated by the use and role of two languages both in the family and in the educational setting.

- Reference is made to the role and status of sign language in policy documents.
- Children and their families have access to deaf adults and BSL from an early stage.
- Both BSL and English are used in live and written forms. They are used in teaching, learning and assessment and are taught as specific subjects.
- BSL and English are kept separate, and are both used in teaching and learning according to the individual needs of the child and the demands of the curriculum.
- Teaching strategies utilise BSL for the development of English skills.
- The language continuum between BSL and English is used flexibly, with English encouraged at the BSL end of the continuum (and vice versa), for use in social and communicative contexts.
- Priority is given to the development of literacy skills.
- Manually coded English may be used to facilitate the development of English and, in specific situations, for curriculum delivery.

Curriculum and assessment

It is recognised that the learning styles and aptitudes of deaf children are different from those of hearing children. Decisions about linguistic support, access to the curriculum and all assessments should be based upon the learning strengths of the child.

Policy issues

In the list of policy issues identified below, emphasis is placed upon assessment and use of a child's first language in curriculum delivery.

- The level of cognitive demand or challenge in teaching should be based upon the child's preferred language and not on their second language.
- The curriculum should reflect a range of languages and cultures including a deaf studies curriculum.
- The development of curriculum-based signs should be in consultation with deaf people.
- Assessment should take account of a child's first language.
- Assessment of need should be based on norms for deaf children and contain references to the child's entitlement to a sign bilingual education.
- Assessment should be ongoing with particular attention paid to deaf children with additional needs or whose pattern of language development is unclear.
- Language specific assessments of BSL and English should be used.

Practice

The issues of practice are also dominated by the use and role of two languages in practice in the classroom, and active discussion about signs within the curriculum between hearing and deaf staff.

- Curriculum assessments are conducted in the child's first language.
- There are agreed presentations for standard assessment tasks and tests.
- Curriculum delivery takes into account the child's preferred language (BSL or English).
- Discussion takes place between deaf and hearing staff regarding the most appropriate signs and register to be used when conveying curriculum content.
- Language specific assessment tasks are available in both BSL and English.

Staffing

All staff should be bilingual, including senior managers (in the sense that they are users of both languages), and reflect the range of educational and linguistic needs of the children. Staffing is the major resource of sign bilingual support and should include the availability of a range of professionals, both deaf and hearing.

Policy issues

Policy issues place emphasis on the essential role of deaf adults, the equality of status among all staff, both hearing and deaf, and the availability of appropriate continual professional development for all staff.

- Native users of both BSL and English should be employed.
- The staffing structure should reflect the equal status of deaf and hearing staff.
- In-service training should be provided to enable all staff to work collaboratively in a bilingual setting.
- Interpreters should be used to ensure there is reflective professional interaction and access for all staff, both deaf and hearing.

Practice

In practice, emphasis is placed upon the active use of both languages with deaf and hearing staff, and training is available for all staff.

- Deaf staff have job descriptions which reflect their positions and status as role models, teachers, etc.
- Deaf and hearing staff are employed in a range of positions.
- Specific in-service training is provided on a regular basis for all staff.
- Procedures are in place regarding the use of sign at times when deaf people are present.

Parents and the deaf community

Policy issues

As in all areas of education, emphasis is placed on parents as equal partners in their children's education, with access to full information allowing them to make informed judgements about their child's education.

- There should be links with the deaf community and other minority communities.
- Children should have access to a community of deaf sign-language users in school and also access to users of English.
- Parents should be well informed about all aspects of sign bilingualism.

Practice

Emphasis here is placed upon easy access for deaf children to a deaf peer group and to members of the deaf community.

- Children have access to a deaf peer group and BSL users.
- Children have access to the deaf community, including social and youth clubs.
- Members of the deaf community are actively involved in the work of the school or service and have the option to become governors.
- Parents are given the opportunity to develop their sign language skills.

As has been said before, it is one thing to develop a policy and consider the practical issues that must be in place before the policy could be said to be fully implemented and quite another to implement it within the variety of educational settings in which most teachers of the deaf find themselves working. There are many variables within deaf education to be considered.

Educational settings

The first is the wide variation in educational settings. This may be within segregated or inclusive settings. There are advantages and challenges to both settings. It is tempting to suggest that it is easier to implement a bilingual model within a segregated setting. It is true that teachers have more control over the content and pace of the curriculum, and are likely to have a viable number of deaf children in a group. However, it is also likely that the first language within the school will be sign language or a sign supported language, and while this is clearly advantageous for developing sign language it may mean that access to English is more restricted. It may also mean that the opportunities for children to access a variety of models of spoken English are also more restricted.

A further issue for a school for the deaf is the wide variation in ability within the group. This is a factor in all educational settings, but it may be exaggerated within a school for the deaf. This is because up to 40 per cent of deaf children are likely to have a difficulty in addition to their deafness, and very often it is those children who have additional difficulties that are placed in segregated settings. It is desirable that children are taught in mixed ability groups, but occasionally the wide variation in ability means that children's work is prepared individually and there can be little interactive learning within the group.

In inclusive settings there are issues around content of the National Curriculum, and the speed with which the curriculum must be covered, and the ability to match this with the needs of deaf children. Within one school this may mean that some children are capable of remaining entirely within the mainstream classes while others will need some extra support on a withdrawal basis. This has implications for the staffing profile.

A great advantage of inclusive settings is the ready access to a hearing community and spoken English and the social experiences and benefits of this, an accurate reflection of the society in which deaf children live. A crucial aspect affecting the success of an inclusive education for deaf children is the commitment of the mainstream school, staff and pupils to sign bilingualism. If it is not fully understood and supported then the advantages of the experience of inclusion for deaf children will be diminished.

Resources

All educational experience is highly dependent upon the resources allocated to the school and the pupils. Resources include human resources such as teachers, communication support workers, and deaf education support workers. They also include suitable teaching spaces and rooms where deaf children can meet and socialise. It is also vital to have support from other services such as audiologists, educational psychologists and speech therapists. To ensure that all of this takes place a firm commitment is required from both the mainstream school and the funding authority.

Linguistic profiles

The varying linguistic profiles of deaf children also has implications for the practice of sign bilingualism. It is true that sign bilingualism, as viewed on a continuum of need, can address the needs of all deaf children, i.e. those for whom sign language is a first language and English is developed as a second language as well as those for whom English is a first language and sign language a second, plus all those between. In reality the difficulties occur when there is a group of children with varying hearing losses and so a likely variation in first language uses and demands. This poses problems for the teacher.

Introduction of English

When and how to introduce English can be an issue. There are strong arguments for not introducing a second language until the first language is well established. This is certainly said to be true in spoken bilingualism, and equally it is the policy advocated in some Scandinavian countries. In reality, in the UK, most deaf children are exposed to English from the earliest days, particularly if they are in a hearing family. Even those deaf children of deaf parents are exposed to English through print, TV and general access to the hearing community. This means that a decision 'to introduce English' is in fact dictated more by the individual child's experiences than by a specific decision by the teacher. What does have to be considered is the timing of a 'structured' introduction of English in terms of developing literacy skills as well as the development of spoken language.

The place of manually coded English systems

The basis of sign bilingualism is the use of two separate languages, in different modalities. In this purist example MCE does not have a place, as it is based on English with borrowed signs from sign language as a support to English structure. While it can be seen that, as it stands, it cannot have a place in a sign bilingual setting, the reality of the classroom suggests that it is a very useful tool. It is certainly a useful tool in the development of literacy skills per se and also as a support for deaf children whose first language is English but who may need some clarification of certain words.

Again the reality of many classrooms is that a cohort of deaf pupils may well have a variety of linguistic profiles, and communication to the whole group may well have to be of the 'best fit' mode, and logically this is some form of MCE.

Positive aspects of working within a bilingual policy

Teachers working in sign bilingual settings were asked to consider what they would see as the positive aspects of working within a bilingual policy. It is extremely heartening and exciting to analyse their responses.

Largely the comments were around language and communication issues, where in general the advantages to deaf children stemming from the opportunity to develop a first or preferred language were outlined in detail, as were the advantages of having varying degrees of access to both languages. Most of the other positive aspects of a bilingual setting followed on from this and included the ensuing opportunities to have access to the curriculum in a preferred language, to work in the curriculum alongside their hearing peers and to work within the same aura of expectation as their hearing peers.

The opportunity for deaf children to be part of a peer group within the mainstream setting was seen as a strength, and staff reported this as contributing to the development of a positive deaf identity. In the past there have been clear indications that, for deaf children educated within the mainstream setting, the advantages academically were clear whereas socially deaf children were disadvantaged. The data collected from mainstream schools seems to suggest that those schools with a significant number of deaf children forming a strong peer group, and particularly those with a strong presence from deaf adults, report a strong feeling of identity within the deaf cohort of students. Clearly for schools for the deaf this is not an issue.

The opportunity for deaf children to meet and interact with deaf adults both as language and role models is also a central issue. This allows the deaf children full opportunity to develop their BSL skills as well as having role models as part of their educational experience. The 'spin off' for the school and hearing pupils and staff is also mentioned frequently, as offering opportunities to learn sign language and to accept deaf students and adults as an ongoing part of school society and thus as a reflection of the wider hearing world. It was felt that a positive attitude was reflected towards deaf children and adults from the hearing world.

In summary, the advantages outlined by sign bilingual provision were seen as holistic and encompassed areas such as communicative competence, equal access to the curriculum for deaf and hearing pupils, the positive development of identity and a positive attitude developing between deaf and hearing children and adults.

The constraints of working within a bilingual policy

In contrast the constraints identified were much more practical and focused primarily upon resources, or the lack of them, in the broadest sense. The lack of training opportunities, the demands of the National Curriculum and the difficulties of providing appropriate support across a wide range of ages and communicative demands within the mainstream setting were the main areas of difficulty and frustration for teachers working within a bilingual setting.

A successful sign bilingual provision depends heavily upon the availability of suitably qualified staff, both deaf and hearing, and upon the staffing level within the setting. Several places commented upon the high level of staff fatigue as a constraint upon their effective functioning. The communicative skill of staff was highlighted as a constraint upon the ability to provide effective sign bilingual support, and this again was linked more to the lack of training opportunities than to willingness of staff to further enhance their skills.

Issues around the demands of the National Curriculum include speed of delivery, the lack of signs needed for some of the curriculum content, and timetabling constraints which precluded the opportunity for pre- and post-tutoring in certain areas.

In summary, the issues related to the implementation of a bilingual policy have been explored in the context of what may be described as an 'ideal setting'. In reality this is hard to achieve, particularly within the inclusive setting. This of course presents a difficult dilemma for teachers and children working within this environment. What is very encouraging is that teachers in general express positive feelings about the advantages of bilingualism and the negative issues relate more to practical issues than to philosophical ones.

Further reading

S. Gregory *et al.* (eds) (1998) *Issues in Deaf Education*, London: David Fulton. There are three chapters describing current policies in deaf education, which clearly outline the different approaches.

PART II

Early Years Context

Of course, effective early years education is a result of team work, involving teachers, nursery nurses, classroom ancillaries, parents and other adults. All have decisions to make and all are involved in translating adult knowledge into childish forms.

(Edwards and Knight 1994: 6)

CHAPTER 4

Pre-School Support

Introduction

Throughout this chapter the terms 'family' and 'parent' will be used to refer to all those people who are closely related to and involved with the child on a day-to-day basis. This would include parents, single parents, the extended family and indeed anybody who could be considered to be in a caring role with the child. These terms will be used interchangeably, but if particular people are referred to in this context then their own title will be used.

This chapter will consider the factors to be taken into consideration in relation to the nature and content of pre-school support programmes within a sign bilingual context. It will focus particularly on the establishment of a productive working partnership between families and professionals and give thought to the family issues which need to be addressed before the introduction of a sign bilingual programme can be made.

Early paths/routes to bilingualism

There is a challenge for teachers of the deaf and all other professionals who are involved in supporting families with a newly diagnosed deaf child within a sign bilingual context. We know that for a small minority, the 10 per cent of deaf parents with deaf children, the path to bilingualism is relatively straightforward. Their children grow up with the opportunity to acquire sign language naturally as a first language, which develops largely in parallel with that of their hearing peers. The path for these children could be described as sequential (Knight and Swanwick 1999) in that they may not be particularly exposed to English in any formal way until school age. The advantage of this is that they are likely to have a well developed first language upon which to build a second. Baker (1995) suggests that bilingualism is then achieved by one of two routes. The second language can be developed as a written language and/or as the vocal form of that language.

For the 90 per cent of children who are born to hearing parents the path or route to bilingualism will not be so smooth, and supporting and encouraging this route is the challenge for all who work with these families. The following are some of the challenges facing those who support these families:

- How to develop a working partnership with parents.
- How to ensure that families are fully informed of the linguistic issues.
- How to build appropriately on the parenting skills of hearing parents.
- How to ensure exposure to wide linguistic experience for the child.
- How to support the development of the sign bilingual child.
- How to develop and support a sign bilingual programme.

Issues for the family

While we appreciate that the development of language is of paramount importance in the life of the deaf child it must be accepted that this presents issues for the whole family. The emotional impact of a family on discovering that they have a deaf child has been well documented (Knight and Swanwick 1999; McCracken and Sutherland 1991; Luterman and Ross 1991). We must expect family reactions to be 'typically and understandably, negative, emotional and very strong' (Knight and Swanwick 1999: 39), although it is important to appreciate that family reactions are individual and variable. Experience and familiarity with the subject would suggest that there will be common factors and the style and manner of support adopted must reflect the needs and profile of each family. For example, Spencer (Spencer *et al.* 2000) reports that in her case study of a family with a deaf daughter, the mother was so relieved to have a diagnosis that she 'hit the ground running' (p. 112), so clearly their needs in terms of support were very specific.

The factors explored above must be acknowledged and accommodated by those who are supporting the families of deaf children. Parents will bring their own background and related issues to any working partnership to be created between the family and involved professionals.

As teachers we accept that the whole family is affected by having a deaf child and that the impact is not just on the child itself. So it is important for the child that the whole family come to some adjustment to the situation, through time and support appropriate to their individual needs, so that they are then able to build on their own parenting skills in a way which is appropriate to the linguistic and social needs of their child.

The following are some reactions from families which are well documented in the literature. It is only by identifying family reactions and responding to them that an appropriate model of support can be developed.

'When I found out my child was deaf, I cried. I couldn't believe it. I was angry too but I didn't know who with.'

'I needed a little time just to let the news sink in.'

'I asked all these questions and then I didn't hear the answers.'

'I remember clearly the absolute devastation.'

'I thought it would help to meet other deaf mums.'

'I wanted someone to chat to who knew about deafness.'

'I saw little girls chattering and thought my daughter will never do that. I didn't think she would ever learn to talk.'

'How am I going to talk to my child?'

'I thought it would help to meet another deaf child.'

'I spent my time crying for what was lost and for not understanding Sophie's problem sooner.'

'I wanted to know if my child would get married.'

'I felt I didn't know how to cope with him any more. It all seemed different.'

(sources: Knight and Swanwick 1999; McCracken and Sutherland 1991; Freeman, Carbin and Boese 1981; Bouvet 1990)

From the reactions described above, a feel for the type of generic support and help a family may be needing begins to emerge, and several dominant threads can be identified. There is no order of priority identified at this point. First, there is the need to allow families *time*. Time to allow an assimilation of and accommodation to all the complex feelings and reactions that emerge. Time to appreciate that these feelings are common, natural; and the time to formulate an appropriate way of articulating them and their reactions to the new situation.

Second, it is important to establish a setting or environment where there is the *opportunity for discussion and sharing of feelings and ideas*, particularly with those other families who have common experiences as well as those who are well informed on all aspects and implications of deafness.

Families' need for the opportunity to acquire *information* on all aspects of deafness is a third factor. There is a wide variety of questions to be answered. Families will want information about a whole range of subjects, such as educational placement, adult life, the biological facts about deafness and what it is like to be deaf. Here it is appropriate to insert a note of caution and to reflect the comments of parents. Lorraine Fletcher (1987), who is the parent of a deaf child, talks about issues of 'information overload' and the balance between wanting information and the ability to retain it. It seems that parents like to have access to information as and when they want, and to select appropriately according to their particular needs at the time.

Fourth, there are concerns about the style of *communication* with their deaf son or daughter and how is it to be established. How is this to be accomplished and what will be the likely outcome for the child? It is well appreciated that this can seem an enormous mountain, particularly at a time when feelings of stress are running high. In fact it is suggested that hearing parents have

> An awesome and unusual challenge of raising a child who experiences the world in a way profoundly different from their own experience of the world.
>
> (Erting 1992: 36)

It is not possible, at the very early stages, to be sure about a child's preferred language. Sign language should be presented as a positive option, but it may also be the case that English will emerge as the preferred language. This is the time to discuss the issues related to the implications of language choice with the parents.

A fifth area of concern is that of *educational provision*. Where children will go to school is an issue of central and immediate concern to all parents of young deaf children, and although it is tempting to suggest that it is too early to discuss these areas most parents are still anxious to know of the various options. At a later stage it is the role of the TOD to offer support in selecting nurseries and schools for their children. Often teachers accompany parents to schools in which they may be particularly interested.

So how can families best be supported during this early time of adjustment? From consideration of family reactions to the situation, the needs of most families can be summed up under the following headings. They may/will need

- time to adjust to the new dynamics within the family;
- the opportunity to talk with a variety of appropriate people;
- full and sensitively delivered information on all aspects of deafness;
- help with developing communication strategies within the whole family and a route to communication with their child;
- guidance through possible education provision.

Gregory (1986) identifies with many of the above needs of parents and adds that whatever the parental reaction, fundamentally, most parents find themselves in a position where they are not sure 'what to do' (Gregory 1986: 51) and their primary need may well be summed up in simple terms. They need to know what to do in the face of these new and unusual circumstances.

Issues for the child

Having considered some of the likely reactions of the wider family, we ask: What are the needs of young deaf children in a hearing family, specifically?

When considering the needs of deaf babies of deaf parents, their needs in the context of social and emotional, physical, cognitive and linguistic development are no different from those of their hearing peers. Their needs will be met naturally within the context of 'good parenting' and 'natural family life' in a home where the significant factors are that the deaf child and their parents share a common language; and that probably there has been little in the way of accommodation to the birth of a deaf child to be made.

If deafness is considered from this perspective it can be seen that it is not the deafness itself which gives rise to a concern but the fact that 90 per cent of deaf children have hearing parents. In terms of language development, the significance is that those deaf children for whom sign language is likely to be the emerging preferred mode of communication are born into an environment where that is not the language used within the home.

The implication of this is that parents and the wider family need to establish a mode of communication which is appropriate for them and for their particular child's needs. The child needs the opportunity to develop their linguistic skills age-appropriately and to be able to interact fully and in a relaxed way with their parents, siblings, peers and the wider community.

> The specific needs of deaf, potentially sign language using children of hearing parents are that they need to be emotionally connected to their parents and to develop fluent communication with them.
>
> (Erting 1994: 37)

There are two significant issues that arise from the above discussion of deaf children's linguistic needs. First, there is a common need for deaf children of hearing parents to have age-appropriate language development, whether the child's potential communication will be in sign language or spoken English. Second, this linguistic need is best met by parents in the home environment, because it is a well established fact that parents have a central and an ongoing role in the language development of their children.

The implication of these two complementary issues is that while we know that parents are the most appropriate people to foster the early language development of their children, this is the precise time that parents may be in need of support themselves. They need the time and opportunity to develop their own skills and the confidence to bring up and enjoy their own deaf child. So the needs of the child are best met within the family setting with appropriate support. Parents should feel reassured that most of what they need to 'know and do' is within normal parenting skills and that it is possible for other new skills to be learnt and absorbed into the parenting role (Knight and Swanwick 1999).

Nature of support to families

There has been a long history of support to the families of newly diagnosed deaf children. It is recognised that the sooner appropriate information and support is given to parents the more successful are the outcomes for the child and the family. For the majority of hearing families it is usually a happening outside their everyday experiences. The family quickly becomes involved in a system where there will be doctors, nurses and audiologists involved. Then, rapidly, the local education authority in the guise of teachers and educational psychologists enters the scene, as do social workers and deaf professionals. While all these people have a positive and a constructive role to play, it is important that parents who will be coping with their own emotions and confusions are not overwhelmed by this wide range of professionals appearing in their lives. Beazley and Moore (1995), who looked carefully at the nature of parents' relationships with professionals, pointed out that it is the nature of support given to families that determines whether or not children's deafness is associated with tragedy.

What is important is that families are aware of the range of possible support available and that they can draw from the support that which best meets their own needs.

The following statements are a general reflection on the areas of which teachers and others should be aware when planning support for families:

- *It is important to ensure that all support offered is based upon and reflects the specific situation of each individual family.*
  Support to families and early years education programmes must be available but should be sensitively planned to allow individualised family support programmes to be developed and implemented.
- *Most deaf children are born to hearing parents who have little acquaintance with deaf people and consequently have little or no knowledge of deafness or the deaf community.*
  The introduction of the family to a deaf adult who will play an important and vital part in the family's life both as a role model and as a sign language user is crucial (see also the role of deaf adults).
- *The practice of always viewing the 'deaf child as member of a hearing family' is potentially a negative concept.*
  The family can be greatly enriched by the experience of having a deaf child. This means that their identity as family with both deaf and hearing members becomes a positive reality (Moores 1996).

- *Support is a whole family issue and should not be directed primarily towards the mother.*
  Support should have built in flexibility that ensures information and discussions about communication are as accessible to fathers and other members of the family as to mothers. Communication should be a whole family issue where all members are encouraged to develop a mode of communication that is successful with the child.

A sign bilingual pre-school support programme

After consideration of the general issues related to early years support the specific policies and practice related to support within a sign bilingual programme need to be incorporated from the beginning.

There are certain practical aspects which should be included in relation to the sign bilingual perspective as identified in *Sign Bilingualism: A Model* (Pickersgill and Gregory 1998).

Language and communication

- Children and their families have access to deaf adults and BSL from an early stage.
- Maximum use is made of amplified residual hearing for the development of spoken language.

Assessment

- Language specific assessments are available for BSL and English.

Staffing

- All staff are bilingual with different language dominances and preferences.
- Deaf and hearing staff are employed in a range of positions.

Parents and the community

- The child has access to a deaf peer group or community of BSL users.
- The child has access to a non-deaf group or community of English users.

Organisation of a support service

The content of this section has been compiled from information taken from a variety of support services.

In general support to children and their families falls into three broad areas. They are:

- support to the family in the home environment
- support in a group situation
- and in some cases support within the hospital setting.

Support in the home

> The positive effect of first visits by teachers of the deaf was reported by parents.
>
> (Powers *et al.* 1999: 156)

The aim of home visiting is to meet the family in a setting which allows for confidentiality and is based within their own familiar territory. Most services aim to visit the family in their home soon after the diagnosis of deafness has been established. Their aim is to be appropriately supportive to the family and to impart information as and when requested. There are certain constraints to imparting information flexibly, and many support services have developed a system of comprehensive handouts which they give in conjunction with verbal information; this has the added advantage of allowing the teacher to keep a track of information given to the family. Others have a policy of giving families comprehensive written information at the start, allowing families the opportunity to look for specific information as and when they need it. It is the right of the family to have full and comprehensive information on all aspects of deafness and it is the remit of the support service to ensure that this happens.

Initial home visits may be made by a TOD, an audiologist or a deaf adult, or any combination of all three. Often the ongoing frequency of visits is negotiable with the family, but some services have found it preferable to establish weekly visits with the option to be flexible depending on the needs of the family. This was because they felt that some families may be reluctant to take up the support offered. Most services were flexible about home visits after the initial input, as often other options such as support groups became more important. Many services agreed to visit in the evenings to ensure that members of the family who worked were not excluded. Visits by deaf adults were usually routine, although some services felt that these visits should be at the request of the family rather than automatic.

Support in groups

Support groups are complementary to and a natural development from a programme of home visiting. They give children the opportunity to interact socially and linguistically with other deaf children – a natural and crucial part of their language development. They allow support given to families to develop into mutual support:

> . . . with the other mums we have a good moan and a good laugh. We are all at different stages or ages . . . it's so good to feel you are not on your own out there.
>
> (Powers *et al.* 1999: 162)

Support groups are a strong element in those services which are not geographically spread out, although one rural service has developed a newsletter which aims to keep families informed and in touch with each other.

Groups take various forms but usually include opportunities for parents and children to meet and interact in a safe and stimulating nursery environment.

Information imparting and sharing, linguistic development, both BSL and English, and most crucially the opportunity for families to meet others who are having or have had similar experiences are all part of the support. Some services provide groups with a language emphasis, such as BSL-focused, staffed by deaf adults:

> BSL group takes place on a weekly basis. Here the children play with deaf 'instructors' in order to develop their BSL skills in a play environment.
>
> (Powers *et al.* 1999: 161)

or English-focused, staffed by speech therapists and TODs:

> a developing English group which any parent or child can attend . . . children are encouraged to use their residual hearing and to develop listening skills. Parents are encouraged to join the group and develop their own listening skills.
>
> (Powers *et al.* 1999: 161)

Families largely respond very positively to the groups. Some of the following are taken from parents in conversation.

'It is vital to meet other parents and not feel isolated'

'Particularly good for child to meet others with a hearing loss'

'We are reaping benefits of going to groups regularly as X's progress is a rewarding thing.'

'It would not be an exaggeration to say they were a life line.'

Of course organising groups is a labour intensive exercise and is also dependent upon families' ability to access them and not be deterred by distance or inaccessibility. Services deal with this in different ways: some offering lifts, some offering fares and others depending upon the mutual support of all members. Some services also offer separate support groups for families of ethnic minority children.

Support in the clinic

Some services have very good relationships with the medical services, and their knowledge and experience of how children are managing hearing aids etc. is a valued and integral part of their work. TODs have found it invaluable to be aware of the type of tests carried out and the results gained, as often parents report being confused and overwhelmed in the hospital situation. This access to clinics gives them the opportunity to clarify issues which parents find difficult. Some services report much less mutual cooperation in this area.

Many services have introduced a 'family plan' or 'educational support plan'. This may come under different titles but the principles are the same. Families should become aware of their own needs and the appropriate support offered to meet those needs and be aware that both sides of the partnership have an obligation to fulfil their roles within the plan.

Roles within pre-school support team

Support teams consist of TODs, deaf adults, speech therapists and audiologists, plus input from educational psychologists, health visitors and others as felt necessary. Not all support services have this amount or pattern of staffing, indeed in some areas there can only be one teacher involved. In other words support is now multidisciplinary in nature.

The role of the TOD

The TOD has responsibility in the following areas:

- establishing a working partnership with parents in the early stages of a child's life;
- offering and making appropriate support available to the family;
- ensuring that families have full information about all aspects of deafness and linguistic and social development;
- ensuring that families have access to the variety of linguistic options;
- contributing to developing a family plan;
- ensuring that there is appropriate monitoring and assessment of children's linguistic and social development;
- ensuring families are well informed about educational placements;
- ensuring a smooth and stress free transition into early years education.

In many situations the TOD becomes the 'key worker' with the family and has a strong liaison role with other professionals.

Free from anxiety about deafness, parents soon learn to communicate freely with their own baby or young child.

(RNID 2001: 5)

The role of the deaf adult

The role of the deaf adult is based upon the characteristics associated with being deaf, such as cultural identity, language use and being a role model (RNID 2000: 28), linguistic skills, and identity as a member of the deaf community in the following areas:

- raising awareness of deafness in all environments
- offering support to parents
- encouraging the development of sign language
- promoting the development of a positive deaf identity in the children.

Parents are introduced to the notion that deafness can be a positive attribute rather than a disabling condition and are provided with information about and experiences associated with the deaf community's own cultural norms.

(Sutherland and Kyle 1993, in RNID 2000: 8)

Other professionals who work or liaise closely with the team offer professional advice and support as and when it is needed.

Monitoring and assessment of children's progress

An important ongoing part of family support is the assessment and monitoring of their child's development. A profile of the child's development, through baseline assessment, is needed to plan an appropriate support programme. All involved people, including the parents, health visitor and teacher of the deaf, should be involved in compiling profiles from which an appropriate support plan can be developed. There must be an appropriate easy and accessible way of recording progress to which all involved people can contribute in an ongoing way. Many of the assessments, and feedback on them to parents, would be considered as ongoing and informal.

The profile of the child's development should give a picture of the whole child's development as well as their linguistic development and should cover at least the following areas:

- hearing aid management
- development of listening skills
- play and early social skills
- development of English skills
- development of sign language skills
- social and emotional development
- development of play skills.

Kungsang (1999) highlights the importance of not over-concentrating on the assessment of linguistic skills at the expense of development of play.

Formal assessments in such specific areas as developing BSL and English skills need to be made by specialists in the area, although contributions to those assessments should be made by all those involved with the child.

The outcomes of assessments form the basis upon which informed choices can be made in relation to the appropriate placement of deaf children into the nursery/foundation stage setting.

Further reading

P. Knight and R. Swanwick (1999) *The Care and Education of a Deaf Child*, Clevedon: Multilingual Matters.

RNID (2001) *Effective Early Intervention for Deaf Children (0–5) and their Families*, London: RNID.

P. E. Spencer, C. Erting and M. Marschark (2000) *The Deaf Child in the Family and at School*, London: Erlbaum.

All the above publications reflect throughout issues related to the early years context.

CHAPTER 5

The Sign Bilingual Nursery/Foundation Stage Department

Introduction

In this chapter, the terms nursery and foundation stage will be used interchangeably. This reflects the current move towards changing terminology in the early years sector of education. It also reflects the current situation where both or either terms are used at ground level in schools and services.

This chapter will consider issues facing teachers and other support staff when they wish to develop a sign bilingual foundation stage setting which will meet the needs of all deaf children. It must be remembered that at the early years stage, for many children their preferred language will not yet be established. This means that access to a broad band of linguistic experiences should continue to be available to all children within the nursery whatever their degree of deafness.

Teachers in nurseries need to be aware of parents' comments. They report that while the support and encouragement they receive during the pre-school years is focused on them as a family, once the child is in nursery or school the focus of support changes from them as a family to the child in school. Support becomes school-based, and home visits and pre-school groups cease to play the same vital role. Those who have felt involved and 'in control' of their child's development have to accept that the shift of control has moved from them to the school. These issues may be exacerbated by the fact that children may be going to a special or resourced school, and this is unlikely to be in their immediate neighbourhood. A further challenge for the nursery is to endeavour to continue to involve and support parents in a meaningful way in their child's school experience.

The aims of nursery/foundation stage provision

need to . . . emphasise the fact that it is probably the first experience a child has of a social setting outside the home.

(Knight 1996: 32)

Before a model of a sign bilingual nursery can be fully addressed some general principles of nursery education need to be established. It is beyond the scope of this book to describe, comprehensively, the philosophy, policy and practice of nursery education, but instead we shall highlight the general aims. It is an environment where the complex needs of the whole child are addressed. For the purposes of this book the nursery setting has been divided into four areas which are not presented in order of importance.

A learning environment

Children need the opportunity to learn through play and an exploration of their environment. This exploration accompanied by a peer group and a more sophisticated learner contributes to an active and productive learning experience. The foundation stage curriculum is commonly used throughout nursery practice, and early learning goals provide the framework for summative assessments.

A physical environment

Children need to develop their own physical potential so that they are able to fully interact with and operate in their own physical environment.

A linguistic environment

Children need the opportunity to continue to develop the linguistic skills they have been gaining in the home environment. There is an assumption, in the context of nursery education, that children do not come to nursery to acquire language but that they come with a language already age-appropriately developed. Although it is appreciated that that is no longer universally true, nevertheless nurseries are largely organised on the basis of an already established linguistic base. Children who come to nurseries with poorly developed linguistic skills are an issue for nurseries. What is also widely accepted is that language development is at its most productive through appropriate interaction with more sophisticated language users, be they adults or peers (Knight 1996).

A social environment

Children have the opportunity to transfer those linguistic skills learned in the home to a broader social setting. Nursery gives children the opportunity to develop and practise their social skills in a wider setting, where the balance of peers to adults may be very different from their home and family experience. It is anticipated that the nursery setting should begin to allow for a gradual move from a socially dependent outlook to a more independent stance. Arguably this is the most important and unique aspect of nursery/foundation stage experience.

The deaf children in foundation stage

While the value of nursery provision cannot be overemphasised, and indeed is entirely appropriate for deaf children, there are a number of factors to be considered. There is a wealth of research evidence to suggest that for deaf children entering nursery it is often the case that

- their first or preferred language development is likely to be delayed;
- their social interactive skills are therefore likely to be less well developed;
- they may therefore be socially and functionally more dependent than other children in the nursery.

This means that the needs of deaf children in a nursery setting may be different from the vast majority of hearing children. Deaf children may be placed in a nursery where many of the linguistic and social skills they need in order to successfully access the usual nursery environment may be underdeveloped. Their primary need may be to continue to develop their linguistic skills to an age-appropriate level.

An interesting and important question to be addressed is the following. If the primary aim of nursery experience for hearing children is as a social setting in which to develop other skills, and the primary aim for deaf children is to develop their linguistic skills, can the same nursery setting meet both these needs? (Knight 1996: 36).

This raises issues of both special and inclusive settings for deaf children, and careful thought needs to be given to how and when placement in a mainstream setting is made and the type of additional support required to meet the deaf child's needs in an inclusive setting.

Whatever form nursery provision takes, the broad aim must be to prepare all children for the demands of the primary curriculum. For the deaf child this means acquiring

- age-appropriate linguistic skills to fully access the primary curriculum
- English skills upon which to base the development of literacy skills
- independent learning skills.

(Knight 1997: 21)

Establishing a sign bilingual nursery environment

The practical aspects which should be included in relation to the sign bilingual nursery programme include the following (taken from *Sign Bilingualism: A Model*, Pickersgill and Gregory 1998). Some of these are a continuation and build on from those practices developed during pre-school support.

Language and communication

- Both BSL and English are used in live and written forms;
- both languages are used in teaching, learning and assessment;
- both languages are taught as subjects and as first or second languages;
- BSL and English are kept separate and both are used within teaching and learning according to the needs of the children and the learning objectives.

Curriculum and assessment

- Curriculum delivery takes into account the child's preferred language (BSL or English).
- A curriculum is available for BSL and English, as first and second/foreign languages.
- Language specific assessments are available for BSL and English.

Staffing

- All staff are bilingual with different language dominance and preferences.
- Deaf and hearing staff are employed in a range of positions: teaching, language and role models, communication support, interpreting, additional needs support and supervision.

Parents and community

- Parents are given the opportunity to develop communication skills with their children; these include the use of sign.
- Information is made available to parents in the home language.

Consideration of the above principles is vital to the establishment of any sign bilingual nursery. The actual situation and set-up may vary considerably depending upon the needs of the children, the facilities and the inclusion policies in the particular area. Usually nursery provision falls into one of three types:

- A deaf nursery where all the children attending the nursery are deaf. These nurseries are often part of a segregated school for the deaf.
- An inclusive nursery where the deaf children are an integral part of the hearing nursery and most of the support offered to them is within the context of the deaf/hearing nursery.
- A resourced nursery where deaf children are placed within a mainstream nursery provision but the school is resourced by both additional staff and usually a room or base where a proportion of the support can take place in a deaf environment.

Practical aspects of sign bilingual nursery/foundation stage provision

Linguistic environment

With sign language, deaf children do not experience any handicap in ensuring the success of their attempts to communicate provided that in this language they have been offered the conditions necessary for language acquisition.

(Bouvet 1990: 145)

A critical and essential feature of the sign bilingual approach is the use of two languages (Powers *et al.* 1999: 207). An important feature of any sign bilingual nursery is that both languages should be available to all the children so that they and the staff are not put in the position of having to make decisions at this early stage regarding children's language choice. It is through this freedom to access both or either of the languages that a child's preferred or first language becomes clear and children's linguistic strengths can be identified.

This language mixing and separation takes different forms in different nurseries, but across the nurseries viewed there were BSL groups and English groups where the language environment was influenced by the staffing. There were also groups with both deaf and hearing staff. It was reported more than once that it is in this BSL/English group that children's language preferences were most clearly identified. Most nurseries were continually adapting and changing the linguistic structure, often in relation to the particular mix of children and/or to meet the requests of parents.

Learning environment

> ... an active exploration of the environment, experience with people, things and language that children acquire knowledge – including metalinguistic knowledge, metacognitive knowledge, and learning to learn.
>
> (Marschark 2000: 285)

It is expected that the learning environment in the nursery will be much as any other nursery in that children will be following the foundation stage curriculum. The difference in a nursery with deaf children will be around the quality and structure of linguistic input and interaction with more sophisticated learners, thus ensuring that all children can fully access the curriculum of the nursery and therefore reach their own learning potential.

> These natural learning processes still rely on an 'implicit pedagogy' that draws children into real learning situations.
>
> (Bouvet 1990: 144)

Social environment

> Both parental and peer relationships are thus essential to social development.
>
> (Marschark 2000: 281)

One nursery highlighted their lunchtime period as the most successful and relaxed opportunity to develop social skills in a wide perspective.

> It is a social time and a very rich source of linguistic opportunity. Many of the linguistic matters ... arise naturally over lunch time ... provides the opportunity to develop appropriate behavioural and social skills. Further there is opportunity for relaxed conversation between adult and children, whilst also allowing children to 'earwig' on adult use of BSL and English.
>
> (Knight 1997: 23)

In resourced nurseries or those which integrate with mainstream children there may need to be an emphasis on awareness of the need to 'encourage' social interaction with hearing peers by, for example, strategically mixing groups for activities.

> Their relationship with peers is also significant for the pupils' experience of the educational process.
>
> (Gregory and Knight 1998: 3)

Staffing

Staff commonly found in nursery provision include the following: teachers of the deaf, deaf adults (the role has different titles in different areas), nursery nurses, bilingual family support workers, speech therapists, audiologists and special needs assistants when appropriate.

All staff need well developed sign language skills to ensure good communication between all members of the team and with all children.

All staff should expect to be involved in observations and recording of children's development. Some special responsibilities are as follows.

Teachers of the deaf

- manage the development of English language skills
- ensure access to good nursery practice
- coordinate an Individual Education Plan (IEP)
- monitor and manage audiological equipment
- liaise with other professionals
- maintain home–school links.

Deaf adults

- develop sign language skills
- are a role model for deaf and hearing children
- maintain home–school links
- promote deaf awareness in the mainstream school
- assess developing sign language skills.

Nursery nurses

- support children in the nursery
- work alongside teachers and deaf adults
- encourage the development of language and learning through play.

Educational audiologists

- support and advise families
- assess hearing loss
- support the management of hearing aid wearing.

Involving parents

Continuing support for parents through groups is common in several nurseries. These are often organised by the parents themselves, who appreciate the opportunity to continue to give each other support as well as having a good knowledge of the provision for their child. It is an opportunity to meet with all the professionals involved with their child and to be well informed of their child's progress. Parents should be involved in the development of Individual Education Plans (IEPs), and copies of these should be either sent home or at least made available for parents to see.

For others who are unable to take advantage of groups due to distance or to other commitments there is the usual weekly or daily 'home book' or other regular communication channel.

Often nurseries incorporate a pre-school play group or parents and toddlers group into their setting. This has the advantage of introducing children and their families to the nursery setting at an early age and certainly helps the transition to nursery for both children and their parents.

Assessment

In all nurseries assessment is an integral part of the day. Teachers and all staff have a role in assessment and can be observed noting down comments in relation to children's language and social development in an ongoing and informal way. BSL linguistic development is usually carried out by deaf staff and English language development by hearing staff. Profiling is a common form of recording development as it is simple and clear, but most foundation stage departments also ensure that they keep evidence of children's achievements.

Models of sign bilingual nursery/foundation stage provision

A strong feature of sign bilingual nurseries (and certainly all nurseries would say the same) seems to be that they are continually reviewing their practice and provision. This means that in the following discussion of specific types of provision it must be accepted they are of the moment, and no nursery provision is ever 'set in tablets of stone' (teacher in conversation).

Sign bilingual resourced nursery/foundation stage provision

A possible model of provision is comprehensively described in Knight 1997. Since this was published there have been many adaptations and innovations within the nursery, including most notably a response to pressure for providing a more specific focus on the development of spoken English.

Resourced nurseries generally have children with a wide range of hearing abilities including children with cochlear implants. This means that for some of them their emerging first and second languages may not yet be clear. For this reason it is important that there is opportunity to have access to both English and sign language throughout the nursery curriculum. Decisions need to be made about which language to use when and with whom. There is also the issue of times when all the children are together, social times and mixed group activities. Those are the times when staff may have to consider some form of sign supported English to best meet the needs of all the children.

A strong advantage of resourced provision is the ease of access to mainstream nursery. This gives deaf children the opportunity to learn with and mix with hearing children in a social setting and have access to ongoing mainstream nursery curriculum and working towards common early learning goals. Also in that setting the spoken and written language of the environment is clearly that of the majority: hearing children.

Segregated nursery provision

Segregated nurseries face many of the same challenges as inclusive nurseries, but the primary difference affecting the organisation of the nursery is that it is likely that most of the deaf children will have sign language as their emerging first language. This has implications for planned language separation in practice. Sign language as a first language and English as a second language is likely to be the reality for the majority of children in a resourced nursery. This gives a clearer structure to language planning and language use.

A possible issue for segregated nurseries is managing experiences of mainstream nursery or indeed working alongside hearing children in the nursery setting. Some nurseries offer places to hearing children in an ongoing way while others have planned access to local hearing nurseries.

Many segregated nurseries have relatively small numbers and therefore a higher staff/child ratio than many resourced nurseries. This also needs careful managing and planning to ensure that children are well and appropriately supported but can also begin to develop the independent learning skills so essential for their future achievements.

In conclusion, sign bilingual foundation stage provision should be based on good nursery practice where access is ensured for all children and programmes are devised to support their developing linguistic needs.

Further reading

P. Knight (1997) 'Bilingual nursery provision: a challenging start', *Deafness and Education* 21(3): 20–30. This article describes one model of a sign bilingual nursery where the policies and practices of sign bilingualism provide the focus for the nursery setting.

D. Bouvet (1990) *The Path to Language*, Clevedon: Multilingual Matters. This book describes in detail the setting up and management of a sign bilingual nursery in France.

PART III

The Classroom Context

we have to understand the structure of deaf children's knowledge so that we can mould our educational methods appropriately ... Academic success is multifaceted and is not predictable from any single variable or combinations of variables. Daunting though it may be, it is time to develop a better model of the deaf learner.

(Marschark 2000: 87)

CHAPTER 6

Language Use in Sign Bilingual Classrooms

Introduction

The growing use of the term 'sign bilingual' to describe deaf children and adults who are bilingual in a spoken and signed language such as English and BSL reflects a more sophisticated understanding of the linguistic needs of deaf children and a growing acceptance of BSL within deaf education. Earlier chapters have shown that the development of sign bilingual educational policy is both recent and ongoing. Information regarding the development of bilingual policy is readily available, but there is currently a need for a greater focus on classroom practice and the outcomes of sign bilingual education. One issue which concerns teachers is how sign language and English (including manually coded English) can best be used in sign bilingual classrooms by the children and the adults. The first national document which fully describes the sign bilingual approach stresses the importance of planned language use according to individual linguistic needs.

> The outcome of a sign bilingual education should be that each child attains levels of competence and proficiency in BSL and English sufficient for their needs as a child and as an adult. The process through which this is achieved should be the planned use of BSL and English before and throughout schooling.
> (Pickersgill and Gregory 1998: 3)

This chapter explores ways in which sign language and English are used in sign bilingual classrooms by both the children and the adults. The descriptions and examples given are drawn from an observational study of sign bilingual classrooms (see Swanwick 2001 for full report). The focus is on the children's language use and repertoire of language skills and the demands of typical teaching activities. Conclusions are drawn about the children's linguistic flexibility, the incidence of language switching and mixing and implications for learning and teaching in sign bilingual settings.

Languages in sign bilingual education

In order to talk about language use in sign bilingual classrooms it is crucial to be clear about terms and definitions. Throughout this chapter the term sign language is used to refer to naturally evolved sign languages which are recognised as distinct from the various sign systems which have been developed to be used alongside spoken language. Because of the different modalities in which sign language and spoken language occur, sign language can be simultaneously combined with the spoken language, and this is referred to as bimodal language use. In an educational context, sign language and spoken language are usually intentionally combined with the goal of making the spoken language more accessible.

There are a number of manually coded forms of English (MCE) which all involve using signs and features from BSL alongside spoken language to support the representation of English. Although these sign codes have been developed to represent English they do not constitute full languages, as neither BSL nor spoken English can be fully replicated using this mode of communication. The term Sign Supported English used here refers to manual representations of English where only some words (usually content words) are signed.

Throughout this chapter we will also talk about language mixing and language switching. In the sign bilingual context the presence of two modalities (sign and speech) and the frequent use of English-based sign codes results in very particular examples of language mixing which are unparalleled in hearing bilingualism, since it is possible to sign and speak at the same time. This is sometimes labelled as contact sign, i.e. the use of sign language which includes elements of both BSL and English as a result of contact and interaction between deaf and hearing people.

There is a distinction between this type of language mixing and the manually coded forms of English that are used particularly for teaching purposes.

What do we know about deaf children's developing sign bilingualism?

In the UK we have not yet looked sufficiently closely at how deaf children respond to a sign bilingual educational experience. The only large-scale project so far into sign bilingual education in Great Britain focused on the attainments and general educational experience of a sample group with reference to the identified goals of sign bilingual education (Gregory, Smith and Wells 1994). Findings from this project were reported in the areas of deaf children's BSL development, their reading, writing and maths attainments, and self-identity.

One of the areas discussed which does give some detailed insight into deaf children's sign bilingual experience is that which considers deaf children's writing strategies and achievements from a second language perspective. In the report of these findings BSL is recognised as the preferred language, and it is acknowledged that written English is likely to be the main means of access to English (Gregory 1997). This aspect of the research considered the strategies the children used for writing and the extent to which their knowledge of BSL influenced their writing, in both positive (facilitative) and negative (interference) terms. Gregory (1997) concludes from analysis of the children's writing errors that deaf children use their knowledge of BSL in their English writing, and argues that this should be considered as a positive, transitional stage which could open up the possibilities of the use of BSL for the discussion of English and how it expresses grammatical information in comparison to sign language. These findings provide food for thought about the ways in which bilingual deaf children's languages interact with each other and the role of one language in supporting the development of the other.

Other research into deaf children's bilingual language development has attempted to explore sign bilingual language development, mainly with the goal of exploring the effect of early sign language acquisition on the development of spoken language. These studies have demonstrated that early sign language acquisition does not prevent deaf children from learning vocal language but can support this process. Also of interest in the review of these studies is evidence of parallel stages of language development across both languages. This suggests that there is evidence of equal competence in both languages and evidence that in a sign bilingual language environment sign language and spoken English can develop in parallel where the potential for the child's spoken repertoire to develop exists. In all of these studies it is important to note that although the subjects studied demonstrate awareness of the separateness of the two language systems, material from both languages is usually mixed in order to fulfil communicative needs. Language mixing and switching, which is characteristic of sign bilingualism, will be further explored in the educational context with reference to the wider field of bilingualism.

Other information regarding sign bilingual language development is often reported incidentally, such as the early language awareness of young sign bilinguals and their ability to argue and debate abstract issues, as well as to be able to identify, for example, language variations between DSL (Danish Sign Language) and Danish.

> They know about some of the differences between spoken Danish and written Danish, and they accept their situation as deaf in a hearing society. They are the first group of deaf children to actually question the way they are approached by hearing people, at the same time as they accept that they are different.
>
> (Hansen 1990: 60)

These benefits have not been systematically researched, but incidentally reported; and yet such observations have crucial implications for sign bilingual children's continuing linguistic, cognitive and social development.

To summarise, research into sign bilingual development so far confirms that the two languages of BSL and English can develop in parallel depending on the access to both languages. It is also evident that the switching between and mixing of languages is common and a normal part of deaf children's language repertoire both for communicative purposes and to support learning. These findings are relevant to all bilingual, not just deaf, children. And yet, what deaf children are having to do differently is develop and move between two modalities and two languages. This is where the experiences of deaf and hearing bilingual children diverge.

> bilingualism in deaf education requires not only learning another language, but also crossing the modality, the basic medium in which the language occurs.
>
> (Neuroth-Gimbrone, 1998: 12)

This chapter looks at the linguistic demands of a sign bilingual setting, how deaf children respond to and cope with these demands and the repertoire of language skills that they demonstrate in such a context. We will discuss ways in which sign language and spoken or written English are used in the sign bilingual teaching context by both the children and the adults.

Language exposure in sign bilingual classrooms

In sign bilingual classrooms deaf children are exposed to a range of linguistic input throughout school life in various different learning situations. The range we identify below is evident across settings both in mainstream schools and in schools for the deaf.

Spoken English

For the purposes of this chapter, the term spoken English is considered to be natural spoken English. This is described as distinct from sign supported English because natural spoken English always involves the use of conventional English grammar whereas the use of English with sign support often does not. Spoken English may be consciously used by the hearing and deaf adults in English teaching situations and for familiar or routine communication throughout the school day. Examples of this include:

- giving familiar classroom instructions; for example,
  Adult: Please shut the door.
- introducing and modelling new words and phrases,
  A: In English the word is 'streamlined'.
- correcting the children's use of spoken English through repetition,

     C: I don't want to say it at Lucy.
     A: You don't want to say it to Lucy? Well, say it to me then.
- asking familiar display questions,
     A: Which one was yellow?
- responding in one word or short phrases to the child's use of spoken English or SSE.
     C: Finished.
     A: Oh, well done!

BSL

In sign bilingual classrooms BSL is usually used by all the deaf adults involved with the children. Hearing teachers of the deaf also use what they refer to as their 'best BSL', being aware of the limitations of their own skills as non-native signers. The term 'best BSL' has emerged recently in this educational context as the hearing teachers have become aware that in some teaching situations the use of BSL is more appropriate than the use of SSE. This has challenged the earlier assumption that all hearing adults should use SSE and deaf adults BSL as both deaf and hearing adults need to be more flexible to meet the needs of the children. The hearing adults are therefore attempting to use BSL but are aware that they lack many of the skills of native signers. The term 'best BSL' therefore indicates that the adult is prioritising visual communication even though the actual BSL is less than perfect. The deaf and hearing adults tend to use BSL and 'best BSL' respectively for parallel purposes such as:

- to explain new concepts and how they are expressed in BSL;
  One example of this was where a hearing adult was telling a story using SSE and the deaf adult intervened to clarify the meaning of <u>cat-flap</u> and give the correct BSL sign.
- to clarify instructions or explanations previously given in English or SSE;
  For example, when the hearing adult asked for the children to underline the words in a text they were unsure of or explained that they were expected to sequence the pictures of a story.
- to clarify English meaning with direct reference to the written form;
  During one reading activity a child was confused by the discrepancy between the written text <u>looked through the window</u> and the one sign given in the BSL version of the story. The deaf adult explained this by giving the BSL translation and then returning to the text to show how English used the two words <u>looked through</u> to express the same meaning which had been conveyed by the one BSL sign.
- to elicit ideas and expand the children's contributions to a discussion;
  This was sometimes done by reminding children of the source or starting point of

the discussion (a story or event) and giving them a little more background information which involved them more directly and personally in the discussion.

- to model new signs and correct individual expressive BSL;
  One example of this was where a child was re-telling a story about a cat that broke some eggs and her initial sign for egg was the sign conveying a broken egg. The deaf adult corrected this, giving her the sign for egg (unbroken) which was contextually correct for that part of the story.

- to model the learning activity and the response;
  In some examples the hearing adult would explain the activity, and this was followed up by the deaf adult showing in detail, by taking on the pupil role, how they would go about the task including the questions they might ask themselves, the materials they would need and particularly how they would start.

- to manage behaviour by intervening.
  Sometimes when a group or individuals were beginning to lose their concentration and disrupt an English-based activity the deaf adult would re-focus the group by gaining all their attention and setting them back on task.

Sign supported English (SSE)

SSE is described as spoken English which is supported by signs in context borrowed from the lexicon of BSL. Sign supported English tends to be used in sign bilingual settings by the hearing adults (with voice), particularly in reading activities:

- reading aloud from text;
  The hearing adult would read from the text aloud and simultaneously produce a sign for each word (often a decontextualised sign).

- clarifying word meanings and explaining the context in more detail;
  The hearing adult would give examples for word meaning and provide more background information but continue to use SSE.

- asking questions about the text;
  This often occurred where children were asked to read some text silently, and then the hearing adult would ask questions using SSE to check their comprehension.

- paraphrasing the English text.
  Sometimes the hearing adult would introduce a new text by summarising what it was about in SSE before reading with the group.

Sign supported English (without voice) may also be used by the deaf adults to read through text with the children and to model the spoken form. For example the deaf adults might take the contextually correct sign from the lexicon of BSL to give the meaning of the English words and to show English word order.

Written English

Despite the potential of written English in sign bilingual classrooms, it is not used a great deal as an actual means of classroom communication (e.g. instructions and explanations) but more generally as a means of introducing words and phrases for the first time with a BSL explanation and also as a means of supporting the children's exposure to spoken English. For example, the introduction of a new written story text might be prefaced by a story-telling activity in BSL which would focus on any new concepts the children were likely to encounter in the text. Also, where the teaching focus is the children's comprehension and use of spoken English, key words and phrases would be written on a flip chart or OHP to support the children's speech reading and speech production. A further strong link to written English is finger spelling, which is predominantly used for the initialisation of names and as an aid for the children to practise and learn the spellings and phonological characteristics of English words.

Language switching and language mixing by the adults

In terms of language switching in sign bilingual settings the hearing adults seem to move between SSE and spoken English quite frequently in English teaching sessions. For example an instruction might be given in spoken English and then the adult will switch into SSE to respond to some written English but move back into spoken English to model specific words or phrases.

Other examples of language switching on the part of the adult include instances where the switch is made from SSE to BSL. This might happen mid-sentence where an adult begins an explanation in SSE then drops the use of voice and incorporates more BSL features into the explanation. This might also happen (less dramatically) mid-session, where an adult begins the session aiming to use as much SSE and spoken English as possible with written support, but the children's need for discussion leads the adult to continue the session in 'best BSL' and abandon some of the English objectives.

The hearing adults also switch languages according to the children's language use. If a child drops the use of sign and begins to use spoken English, the adult will respond in spoken English with the use of sign support. Similarly, where a child moves out of English and pursues something with the adult in BSL, the adult will respond accordingly.

The deaf adults also switch between the two languages but to a lesser degree and for a more limited range of purposes. Deaf adults might switch languages in response to written English. One deaf instructor was observed to read his own text to the children using sign supported English (with no voice) and then to switch immediately back into BSL to gain the whole group's attention and discuss the text. A deaf teacher of the deaf was observed to introduce some written English using BSL questions and explanation and then to switch to SSE (with voice) to model the spoken form.

Language switching by the hearing adults seems to be used primarily to maintain interest and communication. The deaf adults succeed in doing this by remaining with the same language. When the children do not understand, they are able to rephrase and re-explain in BSL or add essential contextual details to their explanation to provide a cue for the children. The constraints that hearing adults are operating within include the potential limitations of their own language skills as well as the linguistic demands of the learning context.

Learning English in a sign bilingual context automatically requires the pupils to move across languages and modes unless the languages are kept strictly separate, and we have so far seen that this is not practical. It is interesting however to look at particular learning activities and analyse the type of switching and mixing demands they engage with on a regular basis. For this purpose three example learning activities are analysed which are considered to be typical but which also reflect the range of teaching approaches observed.

Language switching and mixing by the children – the demands of the learning activities

Example activity 1. Matching English text captions to pictures

For this activity a story is prepared and rehearsed in BSL by the deaf adult and then the children are asked to match English sentences to a sequence of pictures of the story and then read the story back to the hearing adult. This activity has a twofold demand depending on the learner. For the more able reader it involves skimming and scanning for key content words and for the gist of each caption. For the less able reader it entails reading 'aloud' in SSE with the adult and then extracting the key points to complete the text-matching activity.

This type of language mixing in the context of a reading activity has been the focus of discussions about reading instruction for deaf children for as long as sign language has been used in schools. Many teachers feel that reading silently places fewer demands on the deaf reader since it bypasses the need to provide a BSL translation for each written word. An alternative view is that reading aloud using SSE is a necessary stage in reading development. What we need to know is the extent to which this type of language mixing affects the efficiency of the reading process.

Example activity 2. Collaborative writing

For this activity a familiar story is prepared and rehearsed in BSL. The children are then asked to contribute ideas for a group written story which is scribed by a hearing adult. This activity requires the children to contribute to a shared writing activity scribed by the hearing adult who requests that the children express their ideas in SSE or spoken English.

This activity demands that children know some correct English structures and are also able to express them in spoken English as far as possible. The task stretches the children's production, and their participation in the task may be more an indicator of the level of their spoken language skills than their understanding of how English works as a language system. Given that the story is initially prepared in BSL the children are being asked to express the ideas received from the BSL in English and so in effect to translate. This again is a common activity since it is felt that the preparation in BSL supports the children's concept development and contextual understanding. What we do not know is whether or not being asked to switch from BSL to English constrains or supports the contributions they are able to make.

Example activity 3. Comparison of two written English texts

For this activity the children are asked to compare two English texts, one written in the past and one in the present tense. The deaf adult rehearses and consolidates the focus grammar rule using the text in the past tense, and the children are then asked to write their own text using the text in the past tense as a model.

This activity requires the children to take part in a discussion in BSL comparing two English texts. A particular English grammatical rule is highlighted and then a model text is given, full of examples of the rule in use. The children are then required to use the model text to construct their own English version. BSL is used consistently as the language of instruction and for the discussion of English thus giving all the learners an equal opportunity to participate in the discovery of the workings of written English.

This activity differs markedly from the other two examples in that the two languages are used for two very distinct purposes. In activities 1 and 2 both languages are used for the same purpose, either to respond to text or to tell a story. In this example BSL is the only language used for instruction and explanation, and written English provides the example or the subject of that instruction. The children are still being asked to switch languages but it would be interesting to know if this clear demarcation of language use is more supportive of the learning process than the language switching and mixing used for communicative purposes in activities 1 and 2.

What we can learn from these examples is that in the bilingual classroom we often set up activities which require deaf children to switch between or mix their languages. Compared to their hearing (monolingual) counterparts they are responding to quite complex linguistic demands in order to complete activities which seem relatively straightforward. While accepting that language switching and mixing is a natural part of all bilingual children's repertoire it is still worth noting the extent to which we expect them to move across languages and modes in this way in the classroom setting.

The children's linguistic flexibility

From these observations it seems likely that the children have an understanding of the differences between the two languages and are switching or mixing languages appropriately in different contexts for different purposes. What we cannot account for is whether or not the children have a conscious understanding of the differences or whether they are behaving intuitively. The children are also often in situations where their receptive and expressive English skills are called upon, and this is dealt with by individuals in a range of ways.

We can see that sign bilingual pupils are exposed to a range of linguistic input throughout the school day in different learning contexts, especially in teaching situations where the goal is English and where both BSL and English are being used by two adults. In this situation there is constant movement between the two languages and modes, particularly by the hearing adults although this does not seem to impede the children's comprehension.

The children's ability to accommodate the adults' differing language uses and to move between the languages themselves suggests that they have a certain amount of linguistic flexibility. Although many teachers say that they aim to keep the languages separate the difficulties they have in doing this and the evident abilities of the children to adapt to the language shifting leads us to question whether or not language separation is a valid goal in this setting. If frequent language switching and mixing is a natural part of the daily interaction in this context then should we be worried about language separation?

For the most part it seems that sign bilingual children operate successfully and flexibly within a language learning environment where the goals of language use and the reasons for language switching and mixing are not always clear. Although the children's switching and mixing of languages is mostly purposeful, it would be interesting to know if more explicit markers and explanations of adult language would enhance their language awareness and their ability to separate the two languages.

It is clear that the children have various strategies for coping with the demands of the bilingual situation and we are perhaps only just beginning to appreciate the range of language learning resources that they are able to deploy. More information about their developing strategies would give us greater insight into the processes involved, for a deaf child, learning English as a second language, so that we might extend and build on these identified strengths.

Conclusion: Implications for the teaching of English

Developing deaf children's English skills, whatever their preferred language, remains a priority for all teachers of deaf children. Within sign bilingual settings teachers reject notions of language development delay and are continually seeking to capitalise on individual deaf children's linguistic potential as a basis for the development of their English skills. This requires the planned use of both BSL and English in the teaching and assessment process. This means that the two languages of BSL and English (and all of the contact varieties in between) are working alongside each other, which creates a dynamic and challenging linguistic environment.

Within this context teachers are clearly striving to provide adequate exposure to the spoken form of English for the learners alongside more formal English teaching. While the demands of this for teachers should not be underestimated, this sometimes results in confusion between BSL and English and a less than perfect exposure to English coupled with a less than perfect explanation of the structure of English. The meaningful exposure to spoken English that teachers can provide in the classroom is unlikely to be sufficient to enable the children to develop English skills to the high levels required for success and achievement in the mainstream hearing society. We might therefore need to explore how the written form could be more successfully exploited as the model of English, combined with a more extensive and confident use of BSL to discuss and explain languages.

Further reading

C. Baker (2001) *Foundations of Bilingual Education and Bilingualism*, 3rd edn, Clevedon: Multilingual Matters. Chapter 4 of this book looks broadly at bilingual language development but also discusses the role of code switching. Chapter 13 explores ways in which two languages are used in bilingual classrooms.

F. Grosjean (1996) 'Living with two languages and two cultures', in I. Parasnis (ed.), *Cultural and Language Diversity and the Deaf Experience*, Cambridge: Cambridge University Press. This chapter discusses the language modes used by deaf people and explores the diversity of deaf bilingual language use.

CHAPTER 7

Sign Bilingual Approaches to Literacy Development

Introduction

The focus of this chapter is the role of sign language in the development of deaf children's literacy skills. Barriers to literacy for deaf learners have been well reviewed and there are plenty of reports which illustrate why deaf children experience difficulties in developing literacy skills in the way that hearing children do. However, for teachers working with bilingual deaf children there is little to be found on sign language and literacy relating to either educational outcomes or practical teaching approaches. Since many deaf children use sign language and are learning English as a second or additional language, how best to use sign language and (spoken or written) English for the teaching of English to deaf children is an issue for teachers. This chapter looks at the process of literacy development from a bilingual perspective and explores the notion that sign bilingual deaf children should approach the learning of literacy with established sign language skills through which English language learning can be mediated. The practical issue of how to use both languages in the teaching context and how to bridge the gap between the two languages is discussed, and practical teaching strategies are suggested.

Young children's literacy development

Reading is a complex process of getting meaning from print. It is not a passive receptive activity but an interactive process between the reader and the text that requires the reader to be active and thinking. For a reading task to begin to be meaningful, the reader needs to have an understanding of the language system being used and some background knowledge of the content or topic of the text.

It is generally recognised that fluent readers draw on three main sources of information in order to interpret the text. These sources of information are sometimes known as cueing systems, and a fluent reader is able to draw on all of the following cueing systems to varying degrees, depending on their purpose for reading and their familiarity with the topic of the text.

Syntactic cues are cues that the reader gains from their knowledge of the structure of the language they are reading. The reader can predict what the word on the page is likely to be using their knowledge of the written language and its conventions.

> Syntactic clues are probably the most useful and the most reliable for children learning to read in their first language. Children have a 'feel' for the syntax or structure of their language from a very early age.
>
> (Gregory 1996: 75)

Semantic cues enable the reader to make sense of what they read using their experience of life and their world, or cultural knowledge which is relevant to the particular text.

> As members of the same cultural group and speakers of the same language, we automatically rely on shared understandings . . . Learning to speak a language and consequently to predict that language when reading a text, therefore, is intimately linked with the experiences gained in the language.
>
> (Gregory 1996: 77)

Graphophonic cues are cues that the reader gains from their knowledge of how the spoken language is represented through the written symbols. When the reader meets a new word in a text s/he might sound out the word according to the spelling-to-sound rules to help him/her decode it, or guess using the initial letter sound, or recognise a commonly occurring letter pattern such as 'ing'.

> learning to match symbols to sounds is a confined task. It does not demand the sophistication of needing fluent or colloquial English and consequently gives children confidence.
>
> (Gregory 1996: 66)

Successful readers are able to use all of these cues as they go through a continuous cycle of sampling, predicting and confirming their understanding of a text. Difficulties arise for a reader if they are not able to use any of the cueing systems or if they are making insufficient use of any of these cueing systems. By analysing the reading process in this way we can identify where deaf children may experience particular difficulties.

Deaf children's experience of the reading process

Syntactic cues

To use syntactic cues the reader needs to have a knowledge of the language s/he is reading, which is normally developed through speaking and listening. Because deaf children have limited access to the complete spoken form of English it becomes difficult for them to predict meaning in text based on the structural aspects of the language. Deaf children experience particular difficulties taking cues from essential function words, which sign up the reader's way through the text. Function words hold the text together because they link the content words. Function words include:

- pronouns (*he, she, it, they, his*)
- connectives and conjunctions which link ideas (*and, after, before, unless, if*)
- articles (*a, an, the*).

Another problematic area is the ability to track meaning across chunks of text. Deaf children tend to focus on smaller units of meaning, such as individual words, because they cannot process the cohesive links between sentences. English creates cohesive links or ties in several different ways, and being able to carry an idea right through a text is dependent on the reader understanding the cohesive link between sentences. Two important ways in which English creates cohesive ties are the use of reference words and the use of conjunctions.

Reference words point to something in the text that has already been named or mentioned. They are words such as *he, she, it, here, there, the, this, those* and *that*. Deaf children may not recognise the link between the reference word and the object or person being referred to, and this may impede their ability to follow the sense of what is written through a longer piece of connected text.

Conjunctions link and organise ideas in a text. They are words like *and, but, because, so, unless, although, if, however, therefore*. Some conjunctions indicate a time sequence in a text, and these might be *before, after, later*, and *then*. Conjunctions help the reader to guess what might be coming next in a text and to predict the sort of meaning that will follow. Deaf children may not be familiar with the meanings and nuances that conjunctions bring to a text, and this lack of linguistic experience will hamper their ability to read with understanding and to identify the main ideas within a text.

Several research projects have set out to investigate whether exposing deaf children exclusively to spoken English improves their grammatical skills. The findings suggest that there are no grounds to advocate the exclusive use of either spoken or sign language, but that exposure to both sign language and English has the most significant effect on the deaf child's ability to maximise the grammatical component of reading.

Semantic cues

The reader's knowledge of the world is linked to their knowledge of vocabulary. A vocabulary can be defined as the spoken, signed or written labels that a person has for things in their world. Our knowledge of the world is gained through information from spoken, written or signed language. If a beginning deaf reader comes to the reading task with a limited knowledge of the world because of limited early language experiences, then they will have few labels in both languages for the things in their world. If these readers are getting stuck because of lack of relevant vocabulary, then they are probably getting stuck on important meaning-carrying words, which are sometimes called content words. This problem significantly reduces the amount that the reader is able to comprehend and it also reduces the speed at which the reader can process the text. As soon as reading speed is reduced the memory becomes overburdened and less effective as the reader tries to locate an unfamiliar word in their vocabulary store. As a result of this the reading process breaks down into a fragmented and frustrating experience.

Research into deaf children's vocabulary knowledge has demonstrated that deaf children score lower than their hearing peers in vocabulary tests where comprehension of words in isolation is tested. Deaf children perform better in vocabulary recognition tasks where words are in a context and where they meet vocabulary that only has a single meaning. The most significant finding of the research into deaf children's vocabulary is that deaf children seem to have gaps in their signed and oral vocabulary as well as in their written vocabulary. This suggests that vocabulary problems should not just be treated as English problems, instead, the child's general linguistic development and world knowledge needs to be expanded in both sign language and spoken language.

The impact that this area of difficulty has on the child's experience of reading for meaning as a whole is hugely significant, but there are ways in which this can be improved. Success in this area is cyclical in that the bigger the reader's vocabulary the more able s/he is to deal with new vocabulary. Deaf children are often more confident with concrete familiar nouns and action verbs but struggle with abstract and general nouns of which they have less experience. Special efforts have to be made by teachers to expand the deaf child's vocabulary in sign, speech and print beyond the concrete, practical and familiar, and in this way reduce the number of times they get stuck on important meaning-carrying words and so increase their chances of experiencing reading as connected and fluent.

Graphophonic cues

When we introduced the role of graphophonic cues earlier in this chapter we talked about the relationship between sounds and spelling. It would be easy to conclude that making use of these cues is out of the question for many deaf children. Deaf readers may not be able to make use of phonemic information in the same way that hearing readers do, and so they are not able to sound out when they are having difficulty with a newly encountered word. Deaf children may not be clear about how the sounds of speech are represented by letters and clusters of letters and how punctuation relates to the intonation patterns of speech. However, current work in this area has highlighted the need to think in broader terms about phonological skills, which include visual perception abilities, as well as spoken language skills.

Researchers in this field argue that phonological skills are language-based and not just speech-based and that deaf children can develop phonological skills through exposure to sign or spoken language even though their speech ability and auditory experience may be limited.

> the acquisition of phonological knowledge does not exclusively depend on hearing (or residual hearing in the case of deaf individuals). Deaf persons may use information provided by lip-reading, Cued Speech, fingerspelling and even the alphabetic orthography itself to develop a knowledge of the phonological contrasts of oral language.
>
> (Leybaert 1993: 273)

Although this suggests that phonological awareness can be developed through a combination of lip-reading, finger-spelling, articulation and exposure to writing, none of these elements is sufficient on its own to provide the breadth of language experience needed. This multi-channel approach allows deaf children to develop a visual as well as a phonological code. In this way they can then use their visual knowledge of regular spelling patterns to make predictions about words. If deaf children are trained to take advantage of this whole word information, this provides support for whatever phonological information they can use within their auditory limitations. The development of the child's speech reading, articulation skills and use of their residual hearing will contribute significantly to deaf children's overall phonological awareness, but it is important to incorporate work on the visual aspects of phonology so that they have a broader repertoire of strategies for decoding unfamiliar text.

To summarise, deaf children tend to struggle most in the syntactic (grammatical knowledge) and the semantic (meaning, vocabulary and world knowledge) domains, compared with their hearing peers. These problems can be reduced by ensuring that the deaf child has access to rich early language experiences, either through sign language or through spoken language. In the case of vocabulary development, exposure to both sign language and English seems to have the most beneficial effect on their reading development.

Teaching approaches

Teachers working with deaf children for whom BSL is a preferred language are constantly looking for innovative ways to develop their pupils' second language English skills, and this quest is leading us further into the field of second language teaching and learning. These approaches do have a lot to offer since research has shown that deaf people go through similar learning processes and experience similar difficulties in learning English to other second language students. Second language teaching can be broadly grouped into communicative and formal approaches.

Communicative language teaching emphasises the use of the second language for real communicative purposes. It is assumed that while the learners are engaged in meaningful communication the learning of grammar will then happen automatically. Communicative activities are driven by a genuine communicative purpose. The focus of the activities is on the content of the language and not on the structures or grammar used. In contrast, formal language teaching emphasises explained language work where learners are enabled to understand how the language is structured and are given opportunities to practise specific language items. Formal learning gives many students a sense of security and independence, especially at beginner and intermediate levels. Changes in fashion in second language teaching create swings between the formal and the communicative approaches. Generally speaking, experienced learners respond better to formal activities and younger learners respond better to communicative activities but of course the most effective teaching techniques are a combination of both.

Communicative language teaching

Communicative language teaching is based on the premise that successful language learning involves not only a knowledge of the structure and forms of a language, but also the functions and purposes that a language serves in different communicative settings. This approach to teaching emphasises the communication of meaning over the practice and manipulation of grammatical forms.

(Lightbown and Spada 1993: 119)

For hearing children learning a second language, communicative activities provide them with exposure to the language being used for real purposes in real situations.

That deaf children will benefit from using language as a tool for communication in a social context is undisputed, but how can the spoken form be meaningfully used? For some bilingual deaf children, this exposure through speaking and listening is likely to be problematic, depending on their access to the spoken form. Many of the teaching ideas raise complex issues for the teacher of the deaf.

The role of sign supported English

The use of manually coded systems, such as sign supported English, signed exact english or cued speech, is one way of supporting the learner's access to the spoken form. Using one of these systems enables communicative language learning activities such as spoken dialogues and role play to be incorporated into the English teaching programme. Mayer and Wells (1996) suggest that a manually coded form of English would allow deaf children to gain an insight into the spoken form of English, but they agree that manageable ways of actually doing this are far from clear. We know the manually coded English systems are often comfortably used in the home setting where there are deaf and hearing family members, but in a language teaching situation this unique form of language mixing can create some practical difficulties.

One such issue is the validity of speaking and signing at the same time. This has been questioned, as research into this mode of communication suggests that neither the spoken nor the signed message is comprehensible and that this means of communication is not able to fully represent either language in discourse. This assertion is supported by research into the conceptual problems of accessing an auditory language through a visual medium, which found that the amount of spoken message actually represented in the signed message was drastically reduced, resulting in mainly content words being signed and grammar functions neglected (Maxwell 1992).

The arbitrary mixing of the two languages of BSL and spoken English when English is the subject being taught can inhibit the language learner's progress. Swanwick (2001) conducted a pilot study which considered teacher's language use in English teaching sessions and found two factors which seemed to constrain the deaf children's English language learning opportunities. The first of these was that the teacher frequently switched between BSL and MCE throughout the teaching sessions without marking or identifying the switch or language change for the learners. It was also observed that when an English rule or structure was explained to the learners in MCE the spoken English used was restricted and at times incorrect. The use of MCE in these examples was not helpful to the pupils since they either had to search for the spoken English model amidst the frequent language switching and mixings or the model provided was incorrect.

Language separation

Communicative activities should ideally involve the use of spoken English with no manual support, thus ensuring clear language separation and removing the likelihood of learner confusion. This does not mean that no BSL should be used at all but rather that the two languages should have very distinct but complementary roles. Spoken English could be used to provide the learners with a clear model of the target language in use and BSL would be used for very specific purposes which would be made explicit to the pupils, such as:

- to introduce and explain the tasks
- to give the children feedback about their performance
- to keep the children on task (praise and reprimand)
- to discuss an aspect of the structure of the spoken English.

Moving between languages in this purposeful way encourages the learners not to tune out when their second and weaker language is being spoken. Working in this way would enable teachers to draw the learner's attention to how the English language is structured while using it for real communication. Spoken English can be used without sign support to enable bilingual deaf children to experience to some degree the nature of spoken communication. To support this process and take the learners still further the use of written English can also be incorporated.

Communicative writing activities

Written and spoken English can be creatively used together to set up imaginative communicative activities which will improve the deaf learner's access to the spoken form while still avoiding the confusion surrounding the use of MCE in the English teaching classroom. The written form can be used to provide concrete support for listening/watching and speaking activities such as scripts for dialogues or vocabulary/phrase reference sheets for games and role play activities. Text in these examples is not intended to provide the exposure to the spoken form but rather to support and extend the natural spoken exposure. Providing the pupils with the text of what they have seen or heard allows them to see patterns and make links between the spoken and the written word.

The written form also has its own communicative uses and styles which can be explored through particular teaching techniques – the use of dialogue journals or electronic systems such as email, for example – and through its natural inclusion into the language teaching classroom through notes, messages, instructions and letters. The written form is often under-used in bilingual approaches and yet its potential is vast as its use can span both the communicative and the more formal teaching approaches.

Formal language teaching

> Formal language learning [involves] a setting in which second language learners receive instruction and opportunities to practise. In this context, efforts are made to develop the learner's awareness of how the language system works.
>
> (Lightbown and Spada 1993: 121)

Exposure to the spoken form of English in genuine communicative situations may be restricting for some bilingual deaf children. In these cases, more structured and formal approaches to teaching English as a second language may need to be given greater emphasis.

The teaching and learning of grammar

When the language we are introducing involves new grammar it is the language teacher's job to highlight how the grammar works and how it is put together, and this can be done in various ways. One of the most common techniques used is to present the new language in a dialogue or a written text which the students are motivated to watch or listen to, or read, so that they meet the target structures in a meaningful context. The learners need to be given a focus with which to approach the dialogue and a lead in to the new language. For example, they may be asked to note the key points of a written dialogue and to jot down all the plurals they can find. Following the presentation of the new language material the students need to be given opportunities to practise the new structures, and this can be done as an oral or a text activity with deaf children. An explanation should also be given showing how the particular structure is formed. A visual explanation, exploiting the use of colours and charts, makes new language rules more accessible to deaf children. This approach to teaching new grammar is essentially teacher-led.

Another means of introducing new grammar, which may be more motivating for bilingual deaf learners, is the discovery technique (Harmer 1991). This involves giving the students a text and asking them to write down all the instances of the use of a particular grammar rule such as the use of 'a/an' and 'the'. The pupils are then asked to look through their own examples for a pattern or explanation and develop their own hypothesis about how those articles are used. This problem-solving approach does take more time than the teacher-centred explanations, but it involves the pupils in their own learning and is more fun.

Both of these approaches rely on plentiful opportunities for spoken/written prac-tice and on the adult's in-depth knowledge and understanding of the grammar of English and their ability to explain language rules in the child's preferred language. All second language learners need to be taught how language works, how different language structures carry different meanings and how language fits together. Bilingual deaf children will rely more heavily on this information, and so grammar teaching should be a regular feature of their English language programme.

Metalinguistic skills

Another teaching approach employed in sign bilingual settings involves deaf chil-dren's metalinguistic skills and the potential for harnessing these skills in the teaching of reading and writing. Metalinguistic awareness requires an abstract knowledge and understanding of language which involves the ability to think and talk about language, to recognise characteristics of a language and to see how language is structured (Bialystok 1991). For sign bilingual deaf children with limited access to the spoken form of the language they are learning, the develop-ment of metalinguistic understanding provides an alternative means of accessing the written form of English.

Some effective examples of where this approach has been adopted with sign bilingual children are to be found in Sweden and Denmark, where bilingual educa-tion for deaf children is widely accepted. In these countries, Swedish and Danish sign languages (SSL and DSL respectively) are used as the language of instruction and are also taught as curriculum subjects. Emphasis is placed on the learner's continued development of knowledge and skills in SSL and DSL from pre-school level. Learners are expected to be able to analyse sign language and to use it to discuss features of the written second language and to be able to compare and contrast sign language with the written language.

This approach in Sweden incorporates the use of a specially designed set of texts and parallel SSL videotapes that centre on a deaf child and his family. Emphasis is placed on discussion and contrastive analysis of the grammar of the two languages rather than on word-for-word reading of the written Swedish. In this way children are allowed to discover for themselves the contrasting and similar ways in which meaning can be communicated in both languages. The use of signing and talking at the same time (sim-com) is avoided as teachers say that it is easier to talk about two languages when they are kept clearly separate (Davies 1994). In Denmark approaches to literacy teaching also include contrastive analysis and translation work, but spoken Danish is seen as being integral to the development of literacy skills. The use of manually coded Danish for word-for-word reading aloud is accepted as a transitional phase in learning to read.

This approach was further explored in a study by Swanwick (1999). The findings from this suggest that because the deaf children are accustomed to using two languages for learning (separately and mixed) and to moving between the two modalities of sign and text, they do develop an analytical approach to language learning. It was found that deaf children can engage in activities that require analytical and reflective thought about language, even though they may not have age-appropriate competence in both languages. They are able to talk about language and to recognise differences between their two languages. They are also able to manipulate their own language use by switching between or combining their languages, to deal with language tasks.

The role of translation tasks

Given that these skills can be identified, one way to foster the development of deaf children's language awareness would be to take on board some of the more formal translation and comparative analysis work being done with deaf children in Denmark and Sweden. Translation provides an avenue to enhance children's linguistic awareness and their sense of bilingualism. This is particularly pertinent for deaf children whose preferred language does not have a high status in the majority culture. For many bilingual deaf children translation is also a natural everyday activity and therefore it seems sensible to integrate and develop those skills more formally into their English language instruction.

Translation provides the teacher with some insight into how children mentally organise language because it is a demanding activity that draws on the abilities to

- separate the two languages
- comprehend the source material in depth (text or sign)
- analyse the source material (sign or text)
- synthesise the information into target language (written or sign)
- judge the accuracy of the target language product
- be sensitive to/aware of the specific differences between the two language systems.

(Malakoff and Hakuta 1991)

Translation tasks require both metalinguistic and communicative skills because they involve reflecting on language and on language use and then successfully conveying meaning in the target language to another person. Although translation tends to swing in and out of fashion in second language education it could, if it was used appropriately, become a valuable teaching technique with bilingual deaf children. Translation provides these learners with a tangible language task that facilitates greater insight into the workings of their two languages and gives them opportunities to compare and contrast them. It will also enable teachers working in this field to learn more themselves about bilingual deaf children's developing model of English as a second language and how they perceive the differences between BSL and English.

Summary of key teaching issues

The teaching of English as a second language to deaf children does present several issues, which are not insurmountable although they challenge our professional expectations, experience and knowledge:

- The central challenge is to provide the right environment for the learning of English as a second language. To meet this goal we have to address the two conflicting demands of ensuring meaningful and accessible exposure to English for the learner but avoiding the arbitrary mixing of BSL and spoken English.
- With regard to the code-mixing issue, teachers should be mindful of their own language use and be explicit where possible about their separate or mixed use of BSL and English. The children need to be made aware of the differences between the mixed and separate use of their two languages as well as the characteristics of their own mixed language use and the contexts in which this usually occurs.
- In English teaching the children's BSL skills need to become a more holistic and integral part of the process rather than a means to an end. For example, in translation work, more talk in BSL about writing would support the children's concept development and steer them away from writing down the English gloss of the BSL and accepting this as a meaningful translation. Within-language translation work would be particularly helpful as it would broaden the children's language repertoire and enable them to focus on the meaning to be translated rather than the form.

In summary, deaf education should aim to further develop the tacit language awareness which is a result of deaf children's bilingual experience. The role of MCE does need to be spelt out and made explicit to the learners so that it can be used advantageously rather than as a vague 'catch all'. For deaf pupils, given their specific linguistic situation, more emphasis needs to be placed on the development of their awareness of the differences between BSL and written English so that they can begin to appreciate what they can appropriately apply from BSL to the writing task. Alongside this support through discussion in sign language deaf pupils also need planned exposure to the different conventions of written English through wide and guided reading activities. This implies a reading programme which aims to focus the learner's attention on the structures and conventions of written English in addition to developing their individual reading skills. Deaf children's early writing might then be further supported by the use of structured materials such as writing frames and models.

Conclusion

This chapter has discussed the key issues relating to sign bilingualism and literacy and also suggested a number of teaching approaches. Although several challenges have been highlighted, language and exposure to writing conventions through text provide opportunities to compensate for the lack of prior literacy experience and full access to spoken English. Deaf children are unique as bilinguals because they have to learn to operate in two language modes as well as in two languages due to the fact that the ways in which spoken and signed language are produced and perceived are different. We cannot therefore assume that they will be able to transfer skills from their first language of BSL to their second language of English. This means that we have to forge a very specific English teaching model, which continues to build on our understanding of how deaf individuals function as second language learners.

Further reading

E. Gregory (1996) *Making Sense of a New World: Learning to Read in a Second Language*, London: Paul Chapman. This book is written for professionals working with young bilingual children. Part I explores the processes involved in learning to read and write and particular strategies employed by bilingual children and is particularly helpful in enabling us to consider deaf children within a wider bilingual context.

P. Ur and A. Wright (1992) *Five-Minute Activities*, Cambridge: Cambridge University Press; and A. Wright, D. Betteridge and M. Buckby (1983) *Games for Language Learning*, Cambridge: Cambridge University Press. These texts are just two of the many enduring resources for foreign and second language teachers which offer a wealth of fun and short and practical communicative language learning activities. Many of these activities are adaptable for deaf pupils, as the speaking and listening focus can be replaced by reading and writing where appropriate.

CHAPTER 8

Sign Bilingual Deaf Children's Approaches to Writing

Introduction

This chapter provides an overview of the research into deaf children's writing and discusses various writing strategies observed to be used by deaf children. We focus particularly on the role of sign language in the writing process and on the bilingual teaching and learning context. Examples of bilingual deaf children's writing are given which have been drawn from an earlier research project (see Swanwick 2001, 2002). The analysis of deaf children's writing strategies leads to a discussion of the implications for teaching approaches and the use of BSL and English (including manually coded English) in the teaching context.

Errors in writing

Deaf children's attainments in the domain of writing reflect their difficulties experienced with the reading process, which have been discussed in the previous chapter. The focus of research attention has been largely on deaf children's errors in their writing, and these have been catalogued extensively. The most significant areas of difficulty reported are deaf children's limited written vocabulary and insecure grasp of written English syntax. Typical errors reported include

- incorrect use of word order
  example: chocolate cake gone where?
- omission of function words
  example: dog want come with in shop

Explanations for these problems have focused largely on deaf children's early linguistic experiences and access to spoken English, but some researchers have also raised questions about teaching approaches and the extent to which they contribute to deaf children's writing problems. It has been suggested that high levels of teacher management and control that focus on the structure of written English, rather than on pupils' abilities to reflect and discuss, have been identified as constraining deaf pupils' literacy development rather than guiding and facilitating it. Wilbur (2000), for example, identifies teacher focus on sentence structure as a possible explanation for deaf children's stilted writing style, which 'lacks complexity and creativity in terms of temporal sequence' (p. 83).

Only a small number of studies have considered deaf children's writing from a bilingual perspective in that they have sought to identify what is different about their writing abilities and whether these differences are specific to deaf children. This perspective considers that deaf children's errors may be explained by the influence of sign language on their writing and hence provide evidence of an attempt to create their own structures using a language that they already know.

The influence of sign language on the writing process

Some researchers have looked specifically for evidence of the influence of sign language on bilingual deaf children's literacy development. Gregory's (1997) study is one of the few that consider deaf children's writing strategies and achievements from a second language perspective where BSL is recognised as the preferred language and it is acknowledged that written English is likely to be the main means of access to English. This research considered the strategies the children used for writing and the extent to which their knowledge of BSL influenced their writing, in both positive (facilitative) and negative (interference) terms.

The data used was the children's writing of their weekly news, having previously presented it in BSL, and their writing of a story initially viewed in cartoon form. These scenarios provide contrasting information; because in the 'news' situation the children had already prepared and discussed their ideas in BSL, they were therefore being put in a translation situation in that they had to transfer those thoughts, ideas and expressions into written English. The cartoon, however, provided a neutral source, in that no language was used as the preliminary model. Common errors that the children made in their writing were analysed in order to reveal the strategies and processes that the children used to construct their written English. Errors which appeared in the writing of 24 per cent of the children or more were reported as:

- the use of the topic first in a phrase, rather than the subject, followed by a comment, which reflects the structure of BSL;
- the omission of the introduction of the second character, or use of speech marks to indicate interaction between two people, which is indicated in BSL only through the use of body movement or facial expression;

- the introduction of characters followed immediately by what the character says without the English conventions of speech marks and the use of a word such as 'said' or 'answered'. This reflects the ways in which the storyteller can become one of the characters in BSL and sign what s/he did without having to give further explanations.

Gregory concludes from the analysis of the children's errors that deaf children use their knowledge of BSL in their English writing. Gregory argues that this should be considered as a positive transitional stage, which could open up the possibilities of the use of BSL for the discussion of English and how it expresses grammatical information in comparison to sign language.

Through this study, Gregory goes some way to explore the notion of the transfer of skills from a sign language to a written language. However, the theory of transfer between a first (L1) and a second (L2) language remains a problematic issue in the context of sign bilingualism and writing. This problem relates to the role of inner speech in the writing process. The work of Vygotsky (1978) suggests that spoken and written language are interdependent in that spoken language is a bridge from inner speech to written language. Inner speech is seen as an intermediary between oral speech and writing, that is, a means to rehearse, self-direct and mediate between written and spoken forms. Inner speech is associated with oral speech and there is evidence to suggest that deaf children may not have inner speech based on the spoken word but that some may have inner language based on the visual-gestural properties of sign. For these children there is evidence to suggest that their inner language might be a visual-gestural code but we cannot assume that meaning which has been constructed in internal visual-gestural speech can be transferred to linear written language. Areas where deaf children might experience particular difficulties in moving from a mental representation in sign language to the written form would include

- encoding in written English bound morphemes in sign language which are not represented by individual signs but through the manner or style of presentation of the lexical sign;
- representing the signed utterance in the correct English word order since sign language has specific rules about sign order which differ from word order rules in English (in BSL the topic is usually established first);
- capturing the non-manual signals, which convey critical semantic and syntactic information, in printed form;
- providing the context of the meaning, such as the attitude and intention of the characters, which can be conveyed in sign language through the use of facial markers.

Despite the developing research we are still unclear as to how sign language might serve as the mediating function between inner language and written language. In practical terms we still need to know more about how to use both languages in the teaching context and how to bridge the gap between the two languages. As we have seen in the previous chapter, most descriptions of sign bilingual programmes incorporate a strong metalinguistic component, that is, the ability to reflect upon and discuss the properties of both languages is emphasised. Central to these teaching programmes are translation and comparison work between languages, with an emphasis on the development of fluent skills in sign language as L1 and on the written form of the second language. These programmes successfully exploit the strengths of sign bilingualism by using the children's well-developed sign language skills as the medium of instruction. However, they do not fully address the early challenges of learning to read and write, such as the decoding process, the development of phonological awareness and the role of inner language.

The role of manually coded English in the writing process

In search of a more holistic approach to sign bilingual literacy development, which takes into account the role of inner language, some researchers have explored the role of manually coded English in the writing process for sign bilingual children (Mayer 1999; Mayer and Akamatsu 2000). These studies suggest that deaf pupils' development of writing competency benefits where English-based signing is used as an intermediary between American Sign Language (ASL) and written English. It is suggested that English-based signing should have a specific role with regard to preparing for writing rather than become the single mode of face-to-face communication. To complement this, introductory and preparatory work in ASL is suggested, thus supporting the pupils' comprehension and conceptual understanding. These studies suggest that, even for deaf pupils with significant sign language abilities, writing in English involves thinking in English and that this should be supported in the learning environment.

Other research into bilingual deaf children's writing questions whether this would be an appropriate learning route for all and points instead to the role of the pupils' established sign language skills in the writing process. Some studies have explored the use of written glosses for ASL or BSL to support deaf children's English literacy development. It is argued that the writing of an English gloss in response to an ASL or BSL source reflects the pupils' sign language knowledge and hence provides evidence of an attempt to create their own structures using a language they already know. We will explore this notion practically by looking at children's writing later in the chapter.

The relationship between first and second language writing

This question over the extent to which the learner's first language influences their second language writing strategies also extends to hearing learners of English as a second or additional language (L2). In general, research into second language writing concludes that children learn to read and write only once, and that there is therefore a strong relationship between the process of writing in a native language (L1) and writing in a second language. The basic principle proposed is that L1 writing ability provides second language learners with linguistic resources to use as they approach L2 writing. This relationship, sometimes viewed as 'interference', can be more usefully constructed as 'application'. This different perspective emphasises that L2 writers can usefully apply their tacit knowledge of writing in L1 to writing in L2.

In considering bilingual deaf children's experience of writing, we cannot look to their primary experience of writing. They will approach the writing of English without prior experience of learning to write in their primary language and with limited access to the spoken form of the language they are writing down. Although they may have developed sign language as a primary language and have age-appropriate conversational skills, developing literacy proficiency involves learning processes that are qualitatively different from those involved in primary language development. Literacy learning involves higher order processes associated with a reflection upon language structures that are essentially distinct from the primary and universal development of first language competence. Writing is essentially a non-reciprocal activity which depends less on the extralinguistic situation and more on the reflective and deliberate use of text as the source of information.

Individual writing strategies

A closer look at individual bilingual deaf children's writing strategies is needed in order for the role of BSL in the teaching of English to be clarified. Each deaf child brings a diverse repertoire of bilingual abilities to the writing task, and there is no one process which can be applied to all children. It is important to find out how individuals deploy their bilingual skills in particular ways. To illustrate ways in which individual bilingual deaf children tackle the writing process we will draw on in this chapter some deaf children's texts collected and analysed for a previous study (Swanwick 2001, 2002).

Translating from BSL to English

Asking deaf children to translate from a BSL source (e.g. a story) into written English provides some useful insights into ways in which they use their BSL and English in the composing process. This activity also reflects the type of daily language work they do when, for example, something is prepared in BSL and then followed up by a written English activity. The analysis of children writing from this story translation activity revealed a range of individual writing strategies.

Writing a gloss of the BSL

From the analysis of the texts it seems that the children with less well developed spoken language skills tended to write down a gloss of the BSL in response to the translation writing activity. For these children the actual writing was more like the first stage of the translation process. They seemed to accept that certain content words are transferable from BSL to written English but that English requires additional details and linguistic features such as the naming of people and places and the addition of function words. The writing of the gloss of the BSL provided a link from the BSL to the written English, thus allowing them to commence the writing and then incorporate their own English knowledge as appropriate. This supports findings from other studies that stress the value of using a written gloss as an intermediary between ASL or BSL and written English. As can be seen from the example below, the written outcome resulting from this approach includes numerous unconventional English phrases that reflect the structure of BSL. Most notable are the ways in which the topic is often first in a phrase rather than the subject, and the missing subjects before the verbs, leaving us without information which would be explicit in the BSL version.

Text written from BSL story

Hi My little son billy new.
dog want come with in shoP.
better leave house went to shoP look
around idea make chocolate cake.
Chocolate cake leave smell nice
wait for DaDDy at last home
cake gone where dog chocolate
all over his mouth.

Rehearsal in spoken English

For the children with more spoken English skills, the writing down of the English was more like the end of the translation process. It seems that translation for these children takes place internally enabling them to then verbalise their English version before writing. It is likely that the children with more developed spoken language skills have a model of written English that is similar to that of hearing children, which allows them to think in English. These pupils are clearly thinking in English, and as a result their written texts successfully convey the sense of the BSL story but are not hide-bound by the structure of the BSL narrative. Their internal model of English does allow them to be more proficient writers, confirming other similar reports (Mayer 1999; Mayer and Akamatsu 2000). The example illustrates this difference. There are many more conventional English subject/verb structures, the subject is always indicated and there is greater use of articles and pronouns.

Text written from BSL story

"Josh and BiLLy"

Josh got a new dog its NaMe BiLLy.
Josh got a idea for DADDY BirtHday Cake.
BiLLy was HaPPy to buy the Cake.
Josh was waiting for DADDy back
DADDy was back Josh said COME here
there you are it disappear DADDy saw BiLLy
got a chocolate round Billy mouth.

Writing from a picture source

Asking the children to write a story based on a series of pictures provides an interesting contrast with their translation writing and reveals further information about their approaches to writing.

Contrast in complexity

When their texts were compared, the most interesting and unexpected finding was that the children generally used more complex grammar structures in their translation texts than in their picture-source texts.

Characteristically the complex structures found in the translation texts included:

- the use of subordinate clauses such as *Billy was happy to buy the cake*
- complex noun phrases such as *daddy birthday cake*
- connective clauses such as *look around idea make chocolate cake*

By contrast, the structures used in the picture-based texts were more usually short, simple main clauses such as *Chip was happy* or simple clauses without a subject as in *paint the box*, and these were often conjoined by *and* or *then*. The example below of one child's contrasting texts clearly illustrates this.

Another similarity with regard to the children's writing style was the amount of repetition found in the picture-source texts. When the children had to draw on their own English resources to write the picture-based text they seemed to rely more heavily on the repetitive use of the characters' names and on the frequent use of them to conjoin clauses. In the translation text they generally did not repeat themselves in this way. The BSL story source perhaps pushed them beyond their learnt writing strategies and focus on sentence structure, as identified by Wilbur (2000), and challenged their creative use of written English.

Contrast in style

A further interesting challenge for all of the children was how to address the different styles of a written English and a live BSL story and how to convey this in their writing. The children clearly already had strategies for writing an English story from the narrator's perspective. They were aware that they had to identify characters and describe events in a logical sequence and indicate who is doing what. However, the BSL story as the source presented particular problems for their writing because of the discrepancies between the visual and written modalities. In the BSL version the storyteller represented the characters and the subject was rarely named but indicated through role shift and placement.

Some of the children tried to write in the style in which the BSL story was told, in that they told the story as the participator. This is most marked at the start of the story where the deaf narrator sets the scene, and the children attempted to recreate this in their writing as in *Hi My little son billy new dog*. This influence on their writing style continued, with the result that the subject was often omitted or only a single subject was specified for connective clauses in the translation texts, as in *chocolate leave smell nice*. Also, names, subject pronouns and definite and indefinite articles were often omitted in the translation texts, even though the children demonstrated an understanding of their usage in their picture-based texts.

Text written from picture sequence

The big box
Chip and Biff Look at the box.
Biff got a idea. Biff Paint the box.
and mum cut the box.
Chip was Happy Kipper can't see.
Floppy was Happy too. then mum
came then mum was shocked
about the box. Kipper was Happy
Biff was Happy Chip was Happy
again.

The influence of the source on the writing process

Five out of the six children whose texts were collected all produced more examples of correct English in their picture-based texts. Although for most of the children there was not a marked difference in the length of their two texts, most of them attempted more complex grammatical sequences in their translation text than they did in their picture-based text. This is mainly evident through their use of simple and subordinate clauses and simple or complex noun phrases. This finding suggests that what the children have formally learnt about writing English (evident in their picture-based writing) is limited compared to their potential for more diverse and complex written expression.

Implications for literacy instruction

The analysis of the different strategies the individual children used provides some pointers for how to use both languages in the teaching context and how to bridge the gap between the two languages. Ideally, we would like to see all deaf pupils with sufficiently well developed internal models of English which allow them to think in English. However, it is evident from this small sample that this may never be a route for some deaf pupils. Certainly, meaningful exposure to good models of spoken and written English should be a goal in all sign bilingual programmes. This exposure may include the use of some English-based signing, but where this is used its role should be explicitly and clearly defined for pupils and adults. Teachers should be mindful of their own language use and be explicit, where possible, about their separate or mixed use of BSL and English.

In English teaching the children's BSL skills need to become a more holistic and integral part of the process rather than a means to an end. For example, teachers could focus more on concept development and steer them away from writing down the English gloss in translation work; providing more talk in BSL about writing might support the children's use of BSL and accepting this as a meaningful translation. Within-language translation work would be particularly helpful as it would broaden the children's language repertoire and enable them to focus on the actual meaning to be translated rather than the structure.

For deaf pupils, given their specific linguistic situation, more emphasis needs to be placed on the development of their awareness of the differences between BSL and written English so that they can begin to appreciate what they can appropriately apply from BSL to the writing task. For example, the children's approaches to the writing task in this study could have been further supported by discussion of the differences between 'live' story telling (as in the BSL source) and written narrative, since many of the children tried to recreate the sense of 'live' in their writing which caused them problems regarding the use of definite and indefinite articles. Collaborative dialogue in L1 has been found to support other second language learners by enabling them to collectively build knowledge about their L2.

Alongside this support through discussion in sign language, deaf pupils need plentiful exposure to the different conventions of written English through wide and guided reading activities. This implies a reading programme which aims to focus the learner's attention on the structures and conventions of written English in addition to developing their individual reading skills. Deaf children's early writing might then be further supported by the use of structured materials such as writing frames and models. This dual focus – of language awareness raising through sign language, and exposure to writing conventions through text – would aim to compensate for the lack of prior literacy experience and full access to spoken English.

Conclusion

Recreating the conditions for emerging literacy development which is experienced by most hearing children, and on which bilingual hearing children are able to build, is not realistic for deaf children whose primary language is sign language. The goal instead should be to maximise the advantages deaf children's bilingualism affords. This entails building upon their tacit knowledge of languages, resulting from their experience of constantly moving between the different conventions and modalities of BSL and English, and shaping this into a resource for their second language learning.

Further reading

P. V. Paul (1998) *Literacy and Deafness: The Development of Reading, Writing and Literate Thought.* London: Allyn & Bacon. This book explores in depth deaf children's acquisition of English literacy skills. Chapters 5 and 6 discuss and analyse sign bilingual approaches and provide a critical overview of ways in which literacy can be addressed in this context.

CHAPTER 9

Promoting Learning and Access to the Curriculum

Introduction

This chapter focuses on the learning styles of deaf pupils and explores the range of practical skills needed by teachers of the deaf to effectively meet individual learning needs. Throughout this book it is assumed that all deaf pupils benefit from the use of sign language in their education to some degree, depending on their linguistic needs and preferences. All teachers of deaf children should therefore feel confident to work within a sign bilingual or total communication teaching environment and to communicate effectively with deaf pupils and adults. In this chapter the teaching and learning context is therefore viewed from a bilingual perspective, as it is considered that this framework is inclusive of the needs of all deaf children, whatever their preferred language or level of hearing ability.

The policy context

Current government policy stresses two key themes which impact significantly on the education of deaf children. The first is a commitment to raising educational standards for all pupils including those with special needs. This goal remains a priority for all deaf children since research over the last decade shows that deaf children continue to underachieve. Most studies show that in general deaf children are several years behind their hearing peers in their reading achievement. Deaf children do achieve better in mathematics than for literacy, although, in general, their performance is still not on a par with their hearing counterparts. Aside from reading and mathematics, reliable longitudinal data on deaf children's achievements is still not forthcoming, and there is insufficient evidence to demonstrate an overall significant improvement in deaf children's achievements since Conrad's study in 1979. For sign bilingual children the issues are compounded by the extremely limited amount of research into sign bilingualism and the associated need for appropriate assessment procedures and research methodologies.

The second significant government policy is the continued emphasis on promoting inclusion of pupils with special educational needs within mainstream schools. In practice, recent survey figures do indicate that approximately 85 per cent of deaf children are being educated in mainstream schools. It is interesting to consider the implication of this, given that it is currently estimated that 30 per cent of deaf children have a learning disability over and above their deafness. In addition to this there are children in the mainstream primary settings whose hearing problems may not have been identified. This is a frequent occurrence in the case of conductive hearing loss (glue ear), which is known to affect 25 per cent of the primary school population. It is therefore not surprising that, increasingly, mainstream teachers need advice and support in the areas of deaf awareness and the educational implications of a hearing loss.

> Most mainstream teachers feel the need for specific guidance and practical help when a pupil with a significant and permanent level of hearing loss is placed with them for the first time.
>
> (RNID 2000: 5)

The learning styles of deaf children

To begin to address the standards issue we have to look at what we know about deaf children's learning styles. By doing this we are in a stronger position to identify the teaching approaches and educational management needed to maximise their opportunities to succeed. It is argued that deaf children actually think differently from the way in which hearing children do. This does not mean to say that they are not as intelligent or do not understand as well as hearing children, but just that their way of understanding and constructing the world is different. This is thought to be particularly true of children who are brought up using sign language. It is also suggested that in some areas of learning deaf children may be more proficient than hearing children. This view of deaf children underlines a shift towards a much more positive consideration of deaf children as different learners rather than as problem or deviant learners. This contrasts sharply with much of the earlier research into deaf children's cognitive development that focused on their weaknesses rather than on their strengths.

There is a strong history of research into deaf children's intellectual abilities, and the impetus for this was the interest into the link between thought and language. Until recently, research into deaf children's intellectual development was dominated by a deficit model where attempts were made to measure the effects of deafness (seen as simply a sensory deficit) against the norm or standard of hearing people. Deaf children were viewed as linguistically deficient and so used as a natural experimental group to test theories about the influence of language on cognitive development. Some of the early theories about deaf children suggested that they were generally less intelligent than their hearing peers, more concrete in their thinking and less able to deal with abstract concepts.

There were, however, several problems with this early research. There were problems with the research methods used, such as the inability of the researchers to properly communicate the task demands, and the emphasis in the tasks on the children's spoken language skills. These methodological problems disadvantaged the deaf children for whom English was the weaker language, as no account was taken of their sign language skills.

The perspective that prevails today is that the results of tests of cognitive abilities, or intelligence tests, do indicate differences but not deviancies. Marschark explains that deaf children may have 'a different constellation of intellectual abilities' (Marschark 1993: 129). He suggests a variety of reasons why deaf children may not perform as well as their hearing peers on conventional tests of intelligence. He stresses that these differences are not to do with an 'in child' deficit or abnormality, but rather that they reflect deaf children's general lack of experience of learning through interaction with hearing peers and adults. He gives several examples of everyday explicit and implicit learning experiences that deaf children may not encounter or may not be able to access fully, such as:

- a parent's running commentary as they talk their child through a new experience or a change;
- opportunities to gain information and knowledge through incidental and indirect means, such overhearing other child or adult conversations in the classroom, the commentary of the radio or television;
- explicit knowledge gained from direct teaching in the classroom situation.

The key research findings about deaf children's general cognitive abilities can be summarised in two main areas of verbal and non-verbal abilities. Verbal intelligence involves the use of language to solve problems or answer questions. Typical tests include matching vocabulary to pictures, giving opposites or recalling sequences of words or numbers. Non-verbal intelligence does not involve the use of language to solve problems or answer questions. Typical tests include remembering symbols, seeing patterns and sequences and visual discrimination.

Braden (1994) looked at all the studies into deaf children's intelligence and found that there was a remarkable similarity between deaf and hearing scores in intelligence tests. The most significant difference that he identifies is that deaf children's verbal intelligence scores are generally lower than hearing children's are, but that deaf children's non-verbal intelligence scores are exactly the same. It is also interesting to note that deaf children of deaf parents have much higher non-verbal intelligence scores than hearing children. These findings are extremely important when we think about the deaf child in the school setting, as it is clear that they have the same potential to achieve success as hearing children in subjects where non-verbal skills are emphasised, such as in maths and science.

Another significant difference linked to these findings concerns the different development of memory in deaf children. It has been found that deaf children's basic capacity for memory does not differ but that they favour different strategies to recall information. Deaf children's memory for visual information which is presented simultaneously (remembering a map or a plan) is equivalent to their hearing peers. Deaf children's memory for sequential information, which usually requires verbal or spoken rehearsal, is less well developed than in their hearing peers.

It is also suggested that deaf children who use sign language from birth can develop their non-verbal area of intelligence, that is, their ability to organise space and remember spatial concepts, to a higher level than hearing children. This potential must be recognised as a learning strength for deaf children so that their opportunities to achieve success in the whole school curriculum are maximised.

> Deaf pupils should be seen in terms of their strengths, in their ability to access the curriculum through a different modality and even language from other pupils, rather than simply deficient in their ability to hear.
>
> (Watson *et al.* 1999: 41)

If we are to take full advantage of the experience that a deaf child brings to school we need to be aware of these cognitive strengths which visual language can facilitate. Any differences that do exist are therefore not necessarily barriers to adequate functioning in the educational setting. These differences place the onus on teachers' abilities to enable deaf children to develop and use these identified strengths and abilities to their advantage.

Teaching styles

The interaction that deaf children experience in the school context both with adults and with peers is a significant factor in terms of their academic success. How teachers communicate with deaf children was the subject of one of the most significant studies in deaf education to date. This study looked at the structure of interaction in the learning environment. For children to develop language they need to have the opportunity to use it freely and to receive meaningful feedback from those around them. And yet this research found that certain types of teacher interaction actually inhibited the children's language use and their opportunities to contribute in a meaningful way to the conversation.

The research focused on conversations which took place between pupils and teachers in oral/aural settings where all the teachers considered the conversation to be a very significant part of their work in terms of developing the deaf children's spoken language skills. The study explored the notion of control in conversation and found there were different levels of control (see Knight and Swanwick 1998).

It was found that lower levels of control allowed the child to be an active participant in the conversation, that is, to be able to take control of the conversation themselves, contribute readily or introduce new topics. High levels of control, such as requests for repetitions or closed questions, forced the children to respond according to a set pattern or language structure rather than to take part in the conversation. The more control the teacher had over the conversation the more passive and uninvolved the child became. Another effect of the high level of teacher control in the conversation was that the children did not tend to address comments or questions to each other, whereas when the control was low, children conversed and listened to each other.

This research made a considerable impact in the field of deaf education because of the value that teachers of deaf children normally place on conversation and oral interaction as a way of helping children acquire language. The outcomes highlight the fact that some of the learning difficulties are actually a result of the interaction between the learning needs arising from deafness and their learning environment.

The findings from this study are also significant when they are applied to deaf children's experience of learning to read and write. The way in which teachers respond to pupils reading (verbal feedback) and to their efforts with writing (through marking) can be categorised under the same headings of levels of control, and the effects of stifling the child's reading and writing confidence and autonomy are similar.

> teachers may, unwittingly, be limiting children's knowledge of language by keeping their own language too simple. What is needed is greater and more detailed attention to the content and structure of discourse as a basis for linguistic development.
>
> (Wood *et al.* 1986: 168)

Supporting bilingual pupils in a mainstream setting: roles and responsibilities

As well as an appreciation of these teaching and learning issues, teachers of deaf children also need to be practically effective in the varied contexts in which they find themselves working. The role of the teacher of the deaf is a complex one, often requiring them to operate successfully in a multidisciplinary team either within a mainstream setting or within a school for the deaf. As a teacher of the deaf it is important to be able to identify the different aspects of the role and how they link with the role of other members of the team. The make-up of the team often reflects the philosophy and approach of a school or service, particularly regarding the employment of deaf adults and bilingual hearing staff. The central members of any team are likely to be:

- Mainstream Teacher (where applicable)
- Qualified Teacher of the Deaf
- Communication Support Worker
- Deaf Instructor
- Learning Support Assistant

Some services may also have EMAG (Ethnic minority achievement grant) provision:

- Bilingual Worker

Outside agents who are more likely to be attached to the team or school include:

- Educational Audiologist
- Speech Therapist

For any team to operate successfully it is important to be able to identify the *common* and *special* skills of the individuals. It is also important to consider what skills mix a team provides and how individual specialist skills are maximised. In most cases the teacher of the deaf is central to both the teaching and management domains.

These two aspects of the role can, at times, be difficult to reconcile, and yet it is crucial that both are addressed if the overall educational provision is to be coherently and consistently delivered. To address both of these roles a combination of effective teaching, interpersonal and managerial skills are needed. Although this appears onerous, a similar skills mix is required of many other postholders in the mainstream setting (e.g. curriculum area leaders, SENCOs, Key Stage coordinators). The implications of this multifaceted role are that the teacher of the deaf needs to have good interpersonal, managerial and administrative skills as well as curriculum expertise.

Interpersonal skills

For example,

- clear communication with hearing and deaf colleagues
- sensitivity to others' perspectives (mainstream staff, parents, team members)
- successful involvement of parents with pupil learning

- effective mediation between mainstream and unit staff or deaf and hearing staff.

Managerial skills

For example,

- effective deployment of individual skills – respect for others' strengths and weaknesses
- ability to coordinate a diverse team – working to the same goals
- ability to manage meetings (within team, with parents, mainstream staff).

Administrative/organisational skills

For example,

- effective dissemination of important information
- detailed and accessible planning and recording strategies
- effective and meaningful systems for reporting to parents.

Curriculum and pedagogical expertise

For example,

- comprehensive overview of pupils' curricular needs
- essential knowledge of implications of current curriculum development and national strategies (e.g. literacy, numeracy, target setting)
- ability to make appropriate decisions about curriculum delivery for individuals (style, setting, content, materials, language, audiological management).

Given the diversity of the teams working within deaf education it is hardly surprising that the *Review of Good Practice in Deaf Education* identified 'strong leadership and a shared vision as important factors in promoting cohesion and a sense of team' (Powers *et al.* 1999: 215). Good leadership and management were repeatedly identified as central to good practice where managers delegated and empowered others.

Planning, monitoring and assessment

A further crucial area of responsibility for teachers of the deaf is that of somehow coordinating and holding together the information about individual development and learning priorities. The planning, monitoring and assessment cycle facilitates good educational management and teaching which is focused to individual needs. All schools and services now have several layers of planning and monitoring systems which are supposed to ensure that the provision is individually appropriate, good value for money and effective in raising standards.

School and service planning

Teachers of the deaf rarely plan in isolation, and the day-to-day classroom planning should reflect the educational goals and approach of the whole school or service. Current legislation and national initiatives always have an impact on planning both at policy level and in the classroom.

Particularly relevant issues which are likely to affect planning both at whole school/service and at individual levels include the following:

- The current national focus on school self-evaluation and review requires schools to use the outcomes from monitoring and evaluation processes to highlight strengths and weaknesses and thereby identify key areas for future school development. All schools are expected to have in place robust and rigorous systems for monitoring and evaluating the quality of provision (curriculum and teaching) and the progress and standards achieved by pupils.
- The national literacy and the national numeracy strategies are now well established yet still represent two key developments introduced by the government to secure school improvement and to support the achievement of the national literacy and numeracy targets. Both strategies share the two major principles of (1) the daily allocation of time for specific teaching and (2) a detailed planning framework which guides and supports teaching.
- All schools now have a statutory responsibility to set and publish targets in English and Maths which predict achievement by the end of Key Stage 2. This process has highlighted the importance of mapping individual and cohort progress, and most schools now have a management system in place to set annual targets for all pupils. These are generally reviewed mid-way through each year.
- The introduction of performance management builds on established systems of staff development and appraisal in schools. All teachers are included in this process, which focuses on agreeing clear targets related to the overall role of the teachers and, in particular, the progress and attainment of pupils.
- Development planning for special educational needs should take account of the government Green Paper which shares a commitment to raising standards for pupils with SEN by increasing the quality and range of opportunities for inclusion of SEN pupils within mainstream education. A further significant issue is the Best Value review, which is intended to evaluate and compare

services provided by LEAs, including special needs provision and the support provided by specialist teachers and professionals.

- The government has communicated its commitment to providing a successful start for all children's education by promoting comprehensive and integrated approaches to childcare and pre-school education.
- The introduction of the foundation key stage is due recognition of how vital early years experiences are for successful learning. The foundation key stage, which now encompasses the nursery and reception years, outlines a high quality curriculum which builds on what children already know and extends their learning. The early learning goals set expectations for children for the end of the reception year and link clearly into the National Curriculum.
- A system for assessing children at the start of primary schooling (baseline assessment) is well established, and there are now moves towards a national model and approach. The pledge to reduce infant class sizes to below 30 throughout Key Stage 1 remains a prominent issue.
- The introduction of Curriculum 2000, supported by the QCA scheme of work, re-establishes the importance of a broad and balanced education. The progress and attainment of all pupils in all subjects, core and foundation, is now firmly back on the agenda.

In response to these national initiatives effective planning at the whole school/service level should address the following:

- Schools and services for deaf children should be able to demonstrate the impact of provision for hearing impaired children in terms of progress and standards of achievement. Evidence of individual progress should be reflected in annual and end of key stage targets. This will require clarity in planning for the intended learning outcomes and related assessment opportunities to ensure that progress and attainment can be demonstrated.
- Where appropriate, effective systems to measure progress and attainment must be established, for example for BSL development, identity and self-esteem, spoken language development, bilingual language skills. These systems must also be transparent in order to justify the quality and range of support provided.
- For pupils with additional learning needs, levels will need to be identified which reflect achievement in working towards Level 1 or progressing between levels.
- Strategic and financial planning should reflect Best Value and be linked to the whole service development plan. These should reflect on the LEA's Educational and Developmental Plan and the service and school priorities.
- Performance management, which now encompasses the ongoing professional development of all teachers, should respond to the identified skills that

teachers need to demonstrate pupil progress, for example ICT curriculum knowledge, pre-Level 1 targets or approaches to mental maths.

- Whole school/service planning should fully embrace the principle of *inclusion* and incorporate strategies which will provide children with opportunities to work in total or in part within the mainstream context.
- Accurate baseline information will need to be collected, as it is crucial for future target setting. Agreement trialling, moderation and exemplification material will all be essential in this process. Schools and services will need to continue to develop systems for cohort profiling and pupil tracking systems to provide year group information and longitudinal data on each pupil.

Planning for teaching

Curriculum and language planning

Teachers of deaf pupils need to be able to plan for the individual linguistic needs of the pupils across the whole curriculum in addition to their normal curriculum planning. This may include planning for development of English as an additional language (EAL) and coordinating BSL development plans. Planning for individual language needs is an area of expertise of the teacher of the deaf, since the learning needs that are most likely to arise from deafness relate to language and literacy.

> Good planning, based on knowledge of the curriculum, is vital if the way in which a subject is delivered is to be matched to the needs of the pupil.
>
> (RNID 2001: 31)

It is likely that each pupil will need an individual education plan (IEP) for English (spoken and written) and BSL development. These will need to be monitored and reviewed on a regular basis. In the mainstream setting these individual plans should be available for mainstream staff so that they are aware of the linguistic diversity and complexity of learning needs of the pupils they are working with.

Medium-term plans should identify precise learning goals and differentiate between teaching objectives which are curriculum knowledge/skills focused and teaching objectives which are language focused. Medium-term planning for the teacher of the deaf is likely to focus on small groups of children or individuals.

Short-term plans should identify as far as possible which language is intended to be used, when and why. For example, when the teaching goal is curriculum knowledge it may be more appropriate to use BSL. When the teaching goal is recognition of spoken and written curriculum terminology, spoken English with text or sign support might be the best means of providing the supported exposure and recognition practice.

Planning materials

For some deaf pupils, teachers will be planning for their learning needs as second language learners. Within the National Curriculum documentation there is very little that can help with this level of detail, and so teachers will need to draw on other English materials, but reference their planning as far as possible to the NC framework. For BSL there is, as yet, no published curriculum, although there is now a preliminary assessment framework. Some schools and services use a modified version of the National Curriculum speaking and listening levels or adapt other spoken language assessment frameworks (such as the speaking and listening P-levels) for planning and target setting.

Monitoring

Recording pupil learning and progress is also an essential part of the teaching and assessment cycle, which should support future planning. Teachers of the deaf are likely to need to monitor progress in areas of learning additional to the National Curriculum subjects. Areas for monitoring and recording are likely to include

- National Curriculum subjects
- BSL development
- EAL development
- spoken language development
- social and emotional development.

Detailed planning forms the first part of the monitoring and recording process, as clearly identified targets are easier to record against. Monitoring records provide vital information, not only about what a child has achieved, but also about their learning styles or processes. Monitoring is also essential for feedback to parents, other staff and pupils themselves, where appropriate. Monitoring records provide the ongoing evidence of pupil attainment, on which teachers are likely to base assessment and target setting decisions.

When setting up a monitoring and recording system it is important to focus on what the pupils are achieving and not just on what has been taught. It is useful to remember to use observable verbs at the planning stage in the success criteria (e.g. point, pick, say, read, and write) rather than more general terms (e.g. respond, understand, appreciate, and know), which are very difficult to record against. Wherever possible it is useful to set up proformas for recording at the planning stage so that material is not duplicated.

Assessment

Purposes of assessment

Assessment is an integral part of the teaching and learning process which should arise from and inform good practice. A planned programme of assessment for an individual or a group of deaf children should clearly identify what the purpose of the assessment is (e.g. diagnostic, summative or formative).

Diagnostic assessment is concerned with the identification of individual pupils' learning styles and difficulties so that appropriate educational support can be planned. This type of assessment involves identifying the needs arising from hearing loss, particularly with reference to language development, and describing the provision required to meet those needs. This is likely to be linked to the statementing process and baseline decisions about appropriate teaching programmes and realistic targets.

Deaf children's spoken language development is an area where a number of different diagnostic tools are used, and it is important that teachers are familiar with the scope and potential of the assessment procedures used in their setting.

Baseline assessment, which takes place during the first term of reception, is also likely to be used diagnostically. All LEAs are expected to have a framework for baseline assessment which covers language, literacy and social-emotional development. Baseline assessment replaces the 'working towards' element of the National Curriculum and so can provide valuable information for end of nursery reviews and future target setting. Depending on the LEA model available, teachers of the deaf will need to make some modifications so that deaf children's early language development (English and BSL) and language preferences can be effectively monitored through this process.

Formative assessment helps teachers to identify what pupils are ready to learn next. The goal of this type of assessment is to provide information which can be used to decide how a pupil's learning can be taken forward. In order for teachers to be able to decide what pupils are ready to learn next, their current levels of functioning must be considered within a developmental framework which enables teachers to identify existing skills and plan the next curriculum steps. Formative assessment is ongoing and may involve informal procedures, such as monitoring children's learning through questioning or observation, or formal procedures, such as termly or half-termly teacher assessment activities.

Summative assessment provides yearly information about the outcomes of teaching and the overall progress of pupils. This may involve the use of statutory assessment procedures such as end of key stage SATs, or GCSEs, or the use of optional SATs materials or teacher assessment. Teachers of the deaf need to be prepared to deliver or to oversee formal assessment procedures, and this may involve making special arrangements with the relevant exam boards.

Specific guidance for the delivery of SATs to deaf children is incorporated into the relevant QCA handbooks. This guidance has been informed by the work of a national working group which addresses issues such as ways in which the tasks should be presented, the use of BSL for reinforcement and clarification, adaptations needed to worksheets and the use of technical subject vocabulary.

In the current climate, the statutory National Curriculum, baseline assessment and the GCSE exams provide teachers with an assessment framework within which they must operate. To ensure that deaf pupils have equal access to such assessment procedures teachers of the deaf need to be skilled and experienced in

- the appropriate delivery of standardised assessments
- the identification of criteria in areas where additional assessments are needed (BSL, EAL, spoken language skills)
- the identification of criteria for assessing achievements between or before NC levels.

Assessment of English as an additional language
In addition to the above, teachers of deaf pupils may need to develop strategies to assess deaf pupils' achievements in English as a second or additional language (EAL). Current guidance about ways of assessing EAL stresses that although assessment of progress and setting of targets for pupils' EAL needs to recognise differences, these processes should also relate to broader national initiatives.

The following principles of assessing EAL are drawn from the QCA document *A Language in Common: Assessing English as an Additional Language* (2000). These principles are consistent with bilingual educational policy for deaf pupils and can equally be applied to this context.

The principles of assessing EAL
The assessment of English as an additional language should follow the same principles of effective assessment used for all pupils. It should

- recognise what pupils do and reward achievement;
- be based on different kinds of evidence;
- be a valid reflection of what has been taught or covered in class;
- be reliable in terms of enabling someone else to repeat the assessment and obtain comparable results;
- be manageable, both in terms of the time needed to complete the task, and in provision of results which can be reported or passed on to other teachers.

Attention to strengths and weaknesses should be carefully balanced so that there is a positive recognition of a pupil's abilities (summative assessment) alongside information on which aspects of English are most likely to benefit from particular attention (diagnostic assessment). National Curriculum performance should continue to be monitored since it provides important information about the achievements of EAL pupils and indicates what needs to be done to raise achievement further.

Profiling and monitoring attainment
While there remains an issue regarding which scales to use to assess deaf and hearing pupils' EAL achievements, the importance of keeping comprehensive pupil profiles must not be underestimated. Profiles enable teachers to

- recognise the characteristics of pupils' prior attainment, including skills and development which cannot be obtained from numerical data;
- highlight aspects of the curriculum, or of pupils' use of English, which need particular attention when planning the next stages of teaching and learning.

A jointly agreed system of profiling can help class/subject teachers and specialist language support teachers to

- share important information;
- clarify areas for focused work and set targets for learning;
- pinpoint key evidence of teaching and learning across the curriculum;
- plan together effective strategies for pupils' progress towards particular targets, both within the curriculum and for English.

The information gathered through profiling should complement other information obtained through the school's general assessment and monitoring procedures.

The notion of good practice

This chapter has explored some of the issues central to promoting learning, and to deaf children's access to the full curriculum. We have combined a focus on deafness and learning with some of the more practical aspects of the role of teachers. There is clearly no recipe or tool kit to prescribe good educational practice, but certainly some key principles can be identified which are relevant to all settings. We have highlighted the importance of an understanding of deaf children's learning strengths as well as challenges. We have then focused on the role of the teacher of the deaf in ensuring that this information is shared and acted upon. Teachers do often find themselves in the linchpin role, hence the importance of team and interpersonal skills as well as teaching expertise. The *Good Practice Review* (Powers *et al.* 1999) identified this role as a key feature of successful inclusive settings.

> ToDs were identified as playing a significant role in overall school improvement and in promoting whole-school policies.
>
> (p. 216)

Conclusion

One of the greatest barriers to learning can be low expectations of what deaf children can achieve. Teachers of the deaf know that there is no correlation between deafness and intelligence and therefore have to continually promote high expectations of their pupils within the wider educational context. This is particularly pertinent as greater numbers of deaf children are educated within inclusive settings.

> there are a number of factors faced by the adolescent, and children of all ages, who are also deaf and in mainstream schools. These difficulties have nothing to do with deafness itself and in fact are often a consequence of other people's responses . . . and the disabling barriers put by institutions.
>
> (Watson *et al.* 1999: 30)

Further reading

S. Powers, S. Gregory, W. Lynas, W. McCracken, L. Watson, A. Boulton and D. Harris (1999) *A Review of Good Practice in Deaf Education*, London: RNID. This report explores the notion of good practice in the education of deaf children. The areas of focus include support in the mainstream, inclusion, language and social development and the issues surrounding the communication approaches.

S. Powers, S. Gregory and E. D. Thoutenhoofd (1998) *The Educational Achievements of Deaf Children: A Literature Review*, DfEE Research Report RR65, Suffolk: DfEE. This is a major review of the research into deaf children's educational achievements. It identifies the key findings and factors affecting educational achievement.

L. Watson, S. Gregory and S. Powers (1999) *Deaf and Hearing Impaired Pupils in Mainstream Schools*, London: David Fulton. This text focuses on deaf children in inclusive settings. Guidance is offered, through the use of case studies, on teaching, social and communication issues for deaf pupils with a range of linguistic needs.

PART IV

The Current Scene

*Sometimes I think when I became a teacher I accept-
ed a special mission to work on a huge jigsaw puzzle.
Each year the puzzle becomes more and more into
shape, but only after I spend time replacing pieces
that do not fit with ones that do ... It is never too late
to work on the puzzle because it is never done – it just
keeps getting better.*

(Livingston 1997: 159)

CHAPTER 10

Current Issues

Introduction

Sign bilingual education has a firm theoretical base and now has a clearly justified and structured strategy for putting policy into practice. As in any educational practice there are ongoing issues which need highlighting and addressing if the practice is to continue to flourish and develop. Some issues are common to all deaf education philosophies, such as pressures from the National Curriculum, development of the literacy skills of deaf children, appropriate educational placements, the nature of support and appropriate resourcing. However, there are some issues which seem to link more specifically to the sign bilingual context.

Cochlear implants and sign language

Currently the place of cochlear implantation for children who are already developing sign language is an interesting one. There is an assumption that once a child has had an implant then the subsequent support for language development and education should largely reflect the oral/aural approach, but children placed in sign bilingual settings have the same right to be considered for cochlear implantation and the subsequent support as those in oral/aural settings.

The majority of children suitable for implantation are likely to be in the severely and profoundly deaf categories and may be already developing sign language as a preferred language, or their language preference may not yet be clear. In some geographical areas this may not be an option. If the option to develop sign language is there, then the issue of cochlear implants for potential sign language-using children is a very important one.

The issue for sign language-using deaf children, or sign bilingual deaf children, is that the development of spoken and/or written English as a first or second language is of a high priority. If the insertion of a cochlear implant will enhance those skills, then it certainly has a place within sign bilingual education.

The issue is that the rehabilitation programme devised for children with cochlear implants should rightly concentrate on developing the spoken language of deaf children. However, it should not be instead of their developing sign language but should complement it. Currently, new areas of research seem to suggest that deaf children with cochlear implants who use sign language do as well in developing their English skills, and sometimes better than, those deaf children who have only been exposed to spoken language. This would reflect many of the known factors about bilingualism; that is, the development of a second language is enhanced by the firm acquisition of a first language.

A cochlear implant is yet another form of hearing aid and as such cannot restore hearing to normal levels. It has a rightful place, with other amplification devices, in the linguistic and educational development of bilingual deaf children. It maximises the opportunity to develop listening skills and spoken language in deaf children as either their first or second language.

Development of spoken language in the sign bilingual setting

In general, in sign bilingual settings the emphasis is on communication, with spoken language considered as one option within a range of possible communication options. It has been suggested that, in sign bilingual settings, the promotion of spoken language skills is not given the same emphasis as other linguistic skills such as the development of sign language and a concentration on the acquisition of literacy skills. In response to the growing number of children with cochlear implants and to parental wishes, sign bilingual programmes are in general developing comprehensive spoken language programmes, usually in conjunction with speech and language therapists. Often speech and language therapists have undergone some additional specialist training and are heavily involved in assessment of developing spoken language and monitoring of progress.

The implications of the Newborn Hearing Screening Programme (NHSP)

Very early diagnosis of deafness and the subsequent early support to children and families is widely accepted as crucial to successful language development. NHS or newborn hearing screening is the name given to the screening of all new-born babies for significant hearing loss (RNID fact sheet www.rnid.org.uk). This means that support to the family of a deaf child may be in place as early as a few days after birth. This has huge implications for early years support teams in terms of additional professional development and specific training. Services which work within a sign bilingual policy are likely to follow the same principles in relation to support for linguistic development, and support at the early stage, as they would whenever diagnosis is made. That is, parents would be encouraged to expose their child to a wide range of communication options from an early age while also continuing to support the use of the most appropriate amplification systems and the stimulation and development of useful residual hearing.

Audiological support in bilingual settings

Audiological input in relation to the development of residual hearing and listening and spoken language skills of deaf children in sign bilingual settings should be equal to that for deaf children who are educated within an oral/aural approach. This means that the assessment of hearing thresholds, prescription of appropriate amplification and ongoing support for the management of hearing aids should be equally rigorous for all deaf children.

The aim for deaf children who are placed in sign bilingual settings is that of competent sign bilingualism appropriate to the needs of the individual. This may mean that English (or the language of the country where they live) will be their second language. It is their right to have the opportunity to develop their literacy and spoken language skills to their fullest potential. To this end emphasis must be placed on early diagnosis of deafness and full audiological support and appropriate access to and management of audiological equipment and planned acoustic environments in all educational settings.

Training implications

From consultation with teachers in units, resourced schools and schools for the deaf, the major provision issue seems to be a lack of suitably qualified staff. It is not clear whether this is because of a lack of understanding at service and LEA levels about the appropriate staffing levels needed to effectively support deaf pupils in these establishments, or whether it is due to a lack of suitably trained staff. Either way, what is clear is that deaf pupils can only have an effective sign bilingual experience if there are enough suitably qualified staff to carry out the programmes efficiently and productively.

The specific training needs of staff in these settings were identified as increased sign language skills and also further training in developing English skills through the use of BSL. The newly developed sign bilingual consortium aims to identify and support the needs of teachers and others working in sign bilingual settings. There also is a continued need for teachers to be able to attend short courses and workshops and to have opportunities for networking at a national level. This is for all teachers working with sign bilingual pupils and should be part of their continuing professional development.

Deaf teachers of the deaf

Deaf people with the relevant qualifications are needed to apply to train as teachers of the deaf. Their contribution to the education of deaf children is particularly valuable. However, it is well accepted that the route to qualified teacher of the deaf status for deaf people remains a difficult one to follow. A prerequisite for all TOD training is a teaching qualification. The advice is that people who are deaf or hard of hearing should discuss their application and support needs for study with the college or department they are applying to. The earlier they do this, the better (RNID fact sheet www.rnid.org.uk).

This route must be made more accessible, as sign bilingualism depends upon hearing teachers who can sign and deaf adults who are also teachers. In Danielle Bouvet's bilingual class the

> children get to see their two teachers talking with each other. One is deaf, the other is hearing. And each respects the other's way of life. As a team they tell stories that the children enjoy together with their teachers.
>
> (Bouvet 1990: xii)

The way ahead

What is clear is that sign bilingualism is growing in both breadth and depth. In breadth, because sign bilingualism is seen as the way forward by an increasing number of authorities, single schools and single and sometimes isolated teachers. All these people see sign bilingualism as a positive option for all deaf children and essential for those deaf children who will develop sign language as their first language. It is growing in depth as we develop a clearer structure to sign bilingual programmes and are able more efficiently and professionally to address the attendant issues and discover what can realistically be put into practice in schools and in the inclusive classroom. There is a continued need for ongoing evaluation of sign bilingual programmes and, most importantly, longitudinal data collection on individual development and progress.

References

Baker, C. (2001) *Foundations of Bilingual Education and Bilingualism*, 3rd edn, Clevedon: Multilingual Matters

Beazley, S., and Moore, M. (1995) *Deaf Children, their Families and Professionals: Dismantling Barriers*, London: David Fulton

Bialystok, E. (1991) 'Metalinguistic dimensions of bilingual language proficiency', in E. Bialystok (ed.), *Language Processing in Bilingual Children*, Cambridge: Cambridge University Press, pp. 113–40

Bouvet, D. (1990) *The Path to Language*, Clevedon: Multilingual Matters

Braden, J. P. (1994) *Deafness, Deprivation and IQ*, London: Plenum Press

Conrad, R. (1979) *The Deaf School Child*, London: Harper & Row

Davies, S. (1994) 'Attributes for success: attitudes and practices that facilitate the transition toward bilingualism in the education of deaf children', in I. Ahlgren and K. Hyltenstam (eds), *Bilingualism in Deaf Education*, Hamburg: Signum Press

Edwards, A., and Knight, P. (1994) *Effective Early Years Education: Teaching Young Children*, Buckingham: Open University Press

Erting, C. (1992) 'Partnerships for change: creating possible new worlds for deaf children and their families', in *Bilingual Considerations in the Education of Deaf Children*, Washington DC: Gallaudet University Press

Erting, C. (1994) *Deafness, Communication and Social Identity*, Burtonsville, MD: Linstock

Fletcher, L. (1987) *A Language for Ben: A Child's Right to Sign*, London: Souvenir Press

Freeman, R., Carbin, C., and Boese, R. (1981) *Can't Your Child Hear?* London: Croom Helm

Gregory, E. (1996) *Making Sense of a New World: Learning to Read in a Second Language*, London: Paul Chapman

Gregory, S. (1986) 'Advising parents of young deaf children: implications and assumptions', in J. Harris (ed.), *Child Psychology in Action*, London: Croom Helm

Gregory, S. (1997) 'Deaf children's writing: The influence of British Sign Language on written English', paper presented to the International Symposium on Bilingualism, University of Newcastle-Upon-Tyne, April 1997

Gregory, S., and Knight, P. (1998) 'Social development and family life', in S. Gregory, P. Knight *et al.* (eds), *Issues in Deaf Education*, London: David Fulton

Gregory, S., Knight, P., *et al.* (eds) (1998) *Issues in Deaf Education*, London: David Fulton

Gregory, S., Smith, S., and Wells, A. (1994) 'Proceedings of bilingual education seminar', *British Deaf News* (March): 8–10

Grosjean, F. (1996) 'Living with two languages and two cultures', in I. Parasnis (ed.), *Cultural and Language Diversity and the Deaf Experience.* Cambridge: Cambridge University Press

Hansen, B. (1990) 'Trends in the progress towards bilingual education for deaf children in Denmark', in S. Prillwitz and T. Vollhaber (eds), *Sign Language Research and Application*, Hamburg: Signum Press

Harmer, J. (1991) *The Practice of English Language Teaching*, London: Longman

Knight, P. (1996) 'Deaf children in a nursery setting', in P. Knight and R. Swanwick (eds), *Bilingualism and the Education of Deaf Children: Advances in Practice*, Leeds: Leeds University Press

Knight, P. (1997) 'Bilingual nursery provision: a challenging start', *Deafness and Education* 21(3): 20–30

Knight, P., and Swanwick, R. (eds) (1996) *Bilingualism and the Education of Deaf Children*, Leeds: University of Leeds Press

Knight, P., and Swanwick, R. (1998) 'Inclusion of deaf children in mainstream education', *Regional Review* 8(1): 21–2

Knight, P., and Swanwick, R. (1999) *The Care and Education of a Deaf Child*, Clevedon: Multilingual Matters

Kungsang, M. (1999) *Working with Pre-School Hearing-Impaired Children and their Families*, Manchester: Ewing Foundation

Lane, H. (1984) *When the Mind Hears: A History of the Deaf*, New York: Random House

Lane, H., Hoffmeister, R., and Bahan, B. (1996) *A Journey into the DEAF-WORLD*, San Diego, CA: Dawn Sign Press

Leybaert, J. (1993) 'Reading in the deaf: the roles of phonological codes', in M. D. Clark and M. Marschark (eds), *Psychological Perspectives on Deafness*, Hillsdale, NJ: Erlbaum

Lightbown, P. M., and Spada, N. (1993) *How Languages are Learned*, Oxford: Oxford University Press

Livingston, S. (1997) *Rethinking the Education of Deaf Students*, Portsmouth, NH: Heinemann

Luterman, D. M., and Ross, M. (1991) *When your Child is Deaf: A Guide for Parents*, Maryland: York Press

Mahshie, S. N. (1995) *Educating Deaf Children Bilingually*, Washington DC: Gallaudet University Press

Malakoff, M., and Hakuta, K. (1991) 'Translation skills and metalinguistic awareness in bilinguals', in E. Bialystok (ed.), *Language Processing in Bilingual Children*, Cambridge: Cambridge University Press, pp. 141–61

Marschark, M. (1993) *Psychological Development of Deaf Children*, Oxford: Oxford University Press

Marschark, M. (2000) 'Education and development of deaf children', in P. E. Spencer, C. J. Erting and M. Marschark (eds), *The Deaf Child in the Family and at School*, London: Erlbaum

Maxwell, M. (1992) 'Simultaneous communication: the state of the art and proposals for change', in W. Stokoe (ed.), *Simultaneous Communication, ASL and Other Classroom Communication Modes*, Burtonsville, MD: Linstok Press, pp. 67–160

Mayer, C. (1999) 'Shaping at the point of utterance: an investigation of the composing processes of the deaf student writer', *Journal of Deaf Studies and Deaf Education* 4(1): 37–49

Mayer, C., and Akamatsu, C. T. (2000) 'Deaf children creating written texts: contributions of American Sign Language and signed forms of English', *American Annals of the Deaf* 145(5): 394–403

Mayer, C., and Wells, G. (1996) 'Can the linguistic interdependence theory support a bilingual-bicultural model of literacy education for deaf students?' *Journal of Deaf Studies and Deaf Education* 1(2): 93–107

McCracken, W., and Sutherland, H. (1991) *Deaf Ability Not Disability*, Clevedon: Multilingual Matters

Meadow, K. (1968) 'Early manual communication in relation to the deaf child's intellectual, social and communicative functioning', *American Annals of the Deaf* 113: 29–41

Moores, D. (1996) *Educating the Deaf: Psychology, Principles and Practice*, Boston: Houghton Mifflin

Neuroth-Gimbrone, C. (1998) 'Cross modality bilingualism: a curricular framework in education', *LASERBEAM* 30: 12–18

Parasnis, I. (ed.) (1996) *Cultural and Language Diversity and the Deaf Experience*, Cambridge: Cambridge University Press

Paul, P. V. (1998) *Literacy and Deafness: The Development of Reading, Writing and Literate Thought*, London: Allyn & Bacon

Pickersgill, M. (1998) 'Bilingualism: current policy and practice', in S. Gregory, P. Knight *et al.* (eds), *Issues in Deaf Education*, London: David Fulton

Pickersgill, M., and Gregory, S. (1998) *Sign Bilingualism: A Model*, London: Adept Press

Powers, S., Gregory, S., and Thoutenhoofd, E. D. (1998) *The Educational*

Achievements of Deaf Children: A Literature Review, DfEE Research Report RR65, Suffolk: DfEE

Powers, S., Gregory, S., Lynas, W., McCracken, W., Watson, L., Boulton, A., and Harris, D. (1999) *A Review of Good Practice in Deaf Education*, London: RNID

Ree, J. (2000) *I See a Voice: A Philosophical History*, London: Flamingo

RNID (2000) *Deaf Child and Family Intervention Services Using Deaf Adult Role Models: A National Survey of Development and Practice*, London: RNID

RNID (2001) *Effective Early Intervention for Deaf Children (0–5) and their Families*, London: RNID

RNID Education Guidelines project (2000) *Guidelines for Mainstream Teachers with Deaf Pupils in their Class*, London: RNID

RNID Education Guidelines project (2001) *Promoting Access to the Curriculum for Deaf Pupils*, London: RNID

Spencer, P. E., Erting, C., and Marschark, M. (2000) *The Deaf Child in the Family and at School*, London: Erlbaum

Sutherland, H., and Kyle, J. G. (1993) *Deaf Children at Home: Final Report*, Bristol: Centre for Deaf Studies, University of Bristol

Swanwick, R. (1999) 'Deaf children's developing sign bilingualism: Dimensions of language ability, use and awareness', unpublished Ph.D. Thesis, Open University

Swanwick, R. (2001) 'The demands of a sign context for bilingual teachers and learners: an observation of language use and learning experiences', *Deafness and Education International*, 3(2): 62–79

Swanwick, R. (2002) 'Sign bilingual deaf children's approaches to writing: individual strategies for bridging the gap between BSL and written English', *Deafness and Education International* 4(2): 65–83

Ur, P., and Wright, A. (1992) *Five-Minute Activities*, Cambridge: Cambridge University Press

Vernon, M., and Koh, S. (1970) 'Effects of early manual communication on the achievement of deaf children', *American Annals of the Deaf* 115: 527–36

Vygotsky, L. (1978) *Mind in Society: The Development of Higher Psychological Processes*, Cambridge, MA: Harvard University Press

Watson, L., Gregory, S., and Powers, S. (1999) *Deaf and Hearing Impaired Pupils in Mainstream Schools*. London: David Fulton

Wilbur, R. (2000) 'The use of ASL to support the development of English and literacy', *Journal of Deaf Studies and Deaf Education* 5(1): 81–104

Wood, D., Wood, H., Griffiths, A., and Howarth, I. (1986) *Teaching and Talking with Deaf Children*, Chichester: John Wiley

Young, A., Griggs, M., and Sutherland, H. (2000) *Deaf Child and Family Intervention Using Deaf Adult Role Models: A National Survey of Development, Practice and Progress*, London: RNID

Index

Printed in the United Kingdom
by Lightning Source UK Ltd.
107628UKS00001B/345-444